Easy, Fast, and Healthy Meals With the Mediterranean Diet

The Perfect Cookbook for Beginners Who Want to Eat Cleaner, Lose Weight, and Boost Brain Activity

Olivia Perri

Table of Contents

Introduction

Food and culture are joined indistinguishably. We gain great food from our elders, who have gained the same thing from their past age. Along these lines, public plans and tastes are both obtained and acquired, turning into a vital piece of the social character, something that we convey inside us regardless of where we wind up residing. A few families venture to such an extreme as to have their own turns and changes of the conventional dishes that are desirously prepared for all outsiders. Through the miracles of current versatility, societies consolidate more than ever, and various dishes merge, making something totally interesting and endemic.

The Western countries are a wonderful example of national cuisines from all over the world coming together in a single crockpot. Seeing a string of national restaurants right in the middle of a modern metropolis such as Munich is by now a completely ordinary sight, but the fact that one can order and simultaneously eat authentic kebabs and gyros is simply amazing. No matter how different they are, these various dishes still share a common ancestry, one which has been pinpointed as originating from the area roughly surrounding the Mediterranean Sea.

Chapter 1

The Mediterranean Diet

A Brief History of the Mediterranean Diet

Mediterranean cooking alludes to food types eaten in nations that lay inside the districts of the Mediterranean bowl. There are around 22 nations arranged in the Mediterranean bowl, quite: Italy, Greece, and Southern France, all carrying a wide social variety to the menu. There are additional food varieties from Eastern Europe and additional contacts from the Eastern shores of the African mainland. There is no single eating routine, as it is an aggregation of provincial differences. This loans a mixed assortment of ingredients and different approaches to cooking them. The impact of the Mediterranean eating routine started to spread all through the world in the 1950s. The sweltering environment affects the eating routine. With little precipitation, there is little nibbling for dairy cattle. That is the explanation the native individuals of these terrains go to what they can develop. The sun gives them an overflow of rich products of the soil vegetables. Fish additionally assumes a significant part in suppers on the shorelines of the Mediterranean Sea. Solid creatures that can endure dry circumstances, for example, goats and chickens, add to the food also.

The Science behind the Mediterranean Diet

The ever-growing problem of cardiovascular disease is major trouble of the modern Western diet, which increased in the 20th century. The 1970s has been associated with the Western dietary admission of high carb and sweet food varieties. This led scientists to wonder why those living in the Mediterranean regions have such low rates of this deadly condition. The main study in the 1980s was known as the MONICA (Multinational Monitoring of trends and determinants in Cardiovascular disease). It collated over 10 years' worth of data and included 21 countries. The results were so pivotal that they are the foundation of the belief that this is the best diet on the planet. Another study in 2003 took 772 participants, and the tests lasted 3 months. Again, the results showed a larger DECREASE in blood sugar and blood pressure levels, for those on the Mediterranean style diet, than for those on a low-Fat diet. In other studies, the increased consumption of nuts (over a 5year period) has shown a 16-63% REDUCED risk of cardiovascular death. The low mortality rate of those who cook daily with olive oil is just one of the many excellent reasons to change to the Mediterranean way of eating.

Super Health Benefits of a Mediterranean Diet

With the findings of a 30% reduction in heart disease, published in 2013 from a study by the New England Journal of Medicine called PREDIMED, we should take these constant studies seriously. Isn't that inviting enough to encourage you to change your diet? How about the studies that proved Mediterranean foods stop the brain shrinking with age, which has been correlated to the high intake of plant-based foods?

The food on the tables of the Mediterranean basin families is without a doubt more wholesome and nutritious than the typical Western diet. The Ingredients include fish (at least twice a week), providing high Protein along with omega3 Fat. Whilst on the topic of Fats, the olive oil they use comes from the olives they personally cultivate. Olive oil is brimming with monounsaturated unsaturated Fats. These are good Fats with many benefits. One is that it helps reduce the risk of heart disease and strokes. Other foods are outsized portions of vegetables and fruit, nuts, seeds, legumes, and basically any whole grains.

What you will NOT find on their tables are the high in saturated Fats, sugars, and salt processed foods. These foods contribute to the development of cardiovascular disease in the Western diet.

The New Changes Happening When You Are on a Mediterranean Diet

Not only will your heart thank you for the consumption of a Mediterranean style diet, but there are also other changes that will happen to your body:

- Fortify muscles and bones. Studies have shown a 70% increment in strength for the old on a Mediterranean Diet.

- Lower blood sugar levels. Ideal for Diabetes Type II.

- Reduce chances of neurological diseases.

- Eating sound cancer prevention agents diminishes the impacts of cerebrum shrinkage in advanced age.

- Reduce the risk of cancerous cells developing.

- Increase energy and better concentrations skills.

- Helps fight inflammations.

- Get more fit insofar as you screen segment sizes and work out routinely.

- Produce higher paces of dopamine in the mind, prompting a sensation of prosperity and further developed mindset.

- All that vitamin E will further develop skin condition and sparkle.

How to Lose Weight When on the Mediterranean Diet

When you think of pizzas and pasta, you do not associate these foods with weight loss. Whilst you can still eat Carbs on this diet, you will not eat large portions of them. Pasta tends to be a side dish, about a half of a cup, set on a great plate of vegetables and salad.

- The focus on how Mediterranean people eat is not just about the food; it includes such things as smaller portions and exercising. Also, their pace of life is less demanding.

- Feel fuller for longer, as you will be eating more Protein-based Ingredients. This will deter you from eating snacks between meals. However, some relevant snack recipes are included.

- The Ingredients of the Mediterranean-style diet naturally tend to be low in Calories and high in fiber. This is the perfect combination to rid the excess Fat reserves.

- Go for the low-Fat options such as Greek yogurt, milk, and cheese when choosing dairy products.

- Red meat should be consumed only a couple of times a month, if at all. White meats are fine, so long they are the lean options.

- The secret of this way of eating is olive oil. Use nothing else but extra virgin olive oil (EVOO), and you too will live a long and slim life.

Most Useful Tips for Successful Mediterranean Diet

If you can maintain a healthy Mediterranean Diet, the list of health benefits is endless.

- Eating healthier can lead to a longer life. Not only does it increase your lifespan, but it also makes you feel healthier and fitter for longer, well into your golden age.

- This is not a restrictive diet. With our recipes, you will learn that you are eliminating certain types of food from your diet. Yet, with so many remaining, you can enjoy cooking and eating with delight.

- A Mediterranean-style diet is not expensive; after all, it's up to you how much to spend on food and where to buy it. It's pricier to order take-out or to frequent meals at restaurants, so try to limit them.

- You can also go vegetarian and bulk up your meals with legumes, as opposed to having meats. They provide not only ample Protein but also a great amount of fiber.

- As we have said before, and will continue to reiterate, the secret is in the oil. ALWAYS use olive oil. Buy the best you can, and if you can afford it, get the EVOO. If you need an oil that gets hot without smoking, use light olive oil. Your heart will be grateful for the rest of your life.

FAQs

If you are new to this model or want to learn more about it, here are some popular questions:

What is the Mediterranean Diet?

It is a specific diet that removes processed foods and/or foods high in saturated Fats. It's not necessarily about losing weight, but rather a healthy lifestyle choice. It is about ingesting traditional Ingredients consumed by those who have lived in the Mediterranean basin for a long time. Their diets never changed, so they must be doing something right. This is a diet rich in fruits, vegetables, and fish. Cooking with olive oil is a fundamental ingredient and is an ideal replacement for saturated Fats and trans Fats. Vegetables and fruits grow well in the heat of the Mediterranean continents, so it's not surprising that the locals devour plenty of them. Studies show that the people who live in these regions live longer and better lives. Changing your own eating habits to one that is proven to be healthy is a good enough reason to begin.

Is it effective for Weight Loss?

What's the significance here, then to change your dietary patterns to coordinate with Mediterranean food sources? With around 20 unique nations affecting the eating routine, you will have a lot of choices for eating. There are no severe principles, simply adhere to the Mediterranean diet, and it will assist you with shedding those pounds. There is a lot of Protein, assuming you follow the eating routine, which will give you a satisfactory impact. Not just that, a large portion of it makes your body better; no abundance of Fats develop and shipped off the store. Besides, in light of the fact that you feel better, it urges you to practice more. While exercises don't guarantee to help you in getting in shape, they help in numerous alternate ways. As your blood siphons around quicker, your heart can adapt better. Muscles and bones become more grounded. The more endorphins you produce in work out, the better your mindset. In this manner, it isn't just about food; it is about feeling quite a bit better and WANTING to be better.

Menu options aren't difficult, even when you eat out. Choose a Mediterranean-influenced meal with fish or poultry cooked in olive oil. Pile on the vegetables and fruit along with it. Indulge in pasta and pizzas, but in small portions.

Should I Exercise More While on the Mediterranean Diet?

Anyone looking to lose weight should ensure they exercise every day, no matter what their dietary intake is. This does not mean to dash off to a sports club and pay expensive fees. A healthy brisk walk at least twice a week (of at least 6000 feet) takes about an hour. Or 4 x 30-minute energetic exercises, such as walking, swimming, or inventing a home workout. That is the minimum guideline. How much extra exercise you do on top of that depends on how much time you want to spare. Exercise alone does not mean you will lose weight. What you can do, though, is increase your daily Calories by about an extra 200 (if you're on a minimum of around 1600 Calories) on days when you exercise. Already you are doing your heart a great favor by being on a heart-friendly diet. Combine that with basic exercise, and you will have more energy and a healthier body. The Mediterranean Diet, combined with exercise, will help toward losing weight and keep you healthy.

What Foods Should We Eat?

Replacing saturated and hydrogenated Fats with olive oil is one of the major differences in the Mediterranean diet. Everything is cooked in olive oil. That includes salad dressings and marinades. Of course, they grow their own olives in the Mediterranean regions, so it's no surprise this oil is so popular. Other healthy choices include olives and avocados. Primarily, you are increasing your plant-based foods. Don't cook with butter when a recipe asks to use olive oil. Don't use sugar to make foods tasty; use herbs and spices instead. Red meat does not have to be off the menu (prepare only a couple of times every month), but lean white meat is better. Fish is also an important ingredient in this diet and is served at least twice a week.

This quick guide gives an idea of the major foodstuffs. Think of it as a pyramid, with the top Ingredients of the list-making the large foundation. As you go down the list, the pyramid gets smaller, so eat less of these Ingredients:

The foundation of the pyramid consists of being substantial and social. Having family meals, dancing with friends, walking, and sports. These are all activities that people who live in hot climates always do, but all of them play a role in the Mediterranean way of life.

All vegetables, even including tubers (root vegetables. Fruits- from the apple to the sweet fig; dates, grapes, melons, strawberries, bananas, kiwis. Legumes- including peas, lentils, peanuts, chickpeas, and other types of beans. Whole grains- such as oats, rice (wild or brown are better), rye, barley, buckwheat, corn, pasta (whole wheat better), whole-wheat bread (not buttered). Nuts- for example, hazelnut, cashew, walnut, almond (but only a handful daily). Seeds- like the sunflower and pumpkin. Herbs and spices aplenty, with garlic and basil, nutmeg, and cinnamon being the favorites. Also, drink plenty of water.

Seafood and oily fish, from salmon to sardines, and shrimp to oysters.

Poultry, but mostly chicken and duck. Dairy such as Greek yogurt, cheese, and milk. Eggs. Red wine (no more than 5oz daily - if you miss a day, no doing a double). If you don't like alcohol, then drink purple grape juice.

Other meats and sweet things are consumed in small amounts.

What Foods to Avoid

When learning any new diet, it's also important to learn which foods should NOT be included. Another important factor is to read the labels on everything. It is the only way to be completely aware of what goes into your food.

Here's a quick guide for inspiration:

Foods considered as processed, such as sausages and bread, should be eaten in moderation. DON'T have any that are super processed, such as hotdogs, take-outs, pastries. They are exceptionally high in sugars and salt, Ingredients and have proven to be linked to cancer risks.

Check the sugar levels if they are labeled as "low Fat."

STOP adding sugar to your tea and coffee.

ALWAYS check that sugar content is not high on the Ingredients list. The higher it is on the list, the more there is in the food contents. Many readymade foods such as sauces, milk, and even bread have it.

AVOID foods made with refined grains. That means that the process has removed all the important dietary fiber, such as white bread, white flour, white rice, white pasta, etc.

AVOID bad Fats and refined oils. Anything labeled with trans Fats or hydrogenated Fats is bad for you. These can be in foods such as margarine, cakes, even microwave popcorn. Don't use oils such as canola, soy, soybean, etc. outlearn about the types of Fats used in the food you eat, whenever you can. DO NOT buy if "trans Fats" are on the label. Take-outs will not have labels, but they use lots of trans Fats for cooking. BEWARE of them.

Advice on Eating Out?

Just because you enjoy eating at restaurants does not mean you have to ditch the diet. The Mediterranean way of eating positively encourages making meals a social event. It can be a time to get together and unwind. Their way of life might be slower, but there is no reason why you cannot incorporate it into your own new lifestyle. Here are a few tips to help you when eating out:

- As you take a seat, have a glass of water. Studies have shown that drinking 17ounces of water prior to a meal gives you a 44% chance not to overeat, therefore assisting in weight loss.

- Avoid breadbaskets. Eat whole-wheat bread at best, but save that for home and in moderation.

- Avoid fried foods unless you are confident they are cooked in olive oil. The only way to find it is to ask if you're bold enough.

- Skip the appetizer, or share one at the very least.

- For your main course, choose chicken or lean pork if you prefer a meat dish. Or consider having fish instead. Better yet, have a vegetarian plate

- Avoid dishes with sauces. Chances are, they have ample sugar and salt to make them palatable. Again, you could ask, but if you are at a chain restaurant, they may not even know the answer as it comes readymade in bulk. That's not a nice reflection!

- Choose plenty of vegetables, even order more as a side dish.

- Avoid salad dressings.

- Fruit for dessert is always better. If you can't resist a pudding, share it with a few friends; this way, you only have a couple of spoons.

- Enjoy one glass of red wine, and then drink water for the rest of the meal.

- Chew slowly until all the food is masticated and easy to swallow.

- Think about the flavors of your food as you chew. Simply said, don't just eat by design- discover the flavors within.

- Sit down and enjoy the food. Appreciate what you taste and consume

- Restaurant portions may be large, so get into the habit of leaving some food on your plate.

Research Supports the Many Health Benefits of the Mediterranean Diet

The Mediterranean diet's impact on heart health is one of its most commonly studied aspects, and there is copious research demonstrating its positive effect on coronary and vascular function.

In 2011, for example, researchers at the University of Miami published a study on the cardiovascular benefits of following a Mediterranean diet. The results of the study showed that consuming fresh fruit and vegetables, whole grains, olive oil, nuts, and fish was an excellent way to improve heart health and decrease the risk of cardiovascular disease.

Also, in 2011, the journal Public Health Nutrition published the results of a study that demonstrated that the high volume of whole grains consumed in the Mediterranean diet makes it an effective method for reducing the risk of some forms of cancer, particularly colorectal cancer.

Then, in 2012, the Department of Internal Medicine and Geriatrics at the University of Palermo, Italy, distributed the aftereffects of a review that showed that the Mediterranean eating regimen had a positive effect on heart wellbeing, yet additionally on the frequency of diabetes.

And again in 2012, Spanish researchers from the Diabetes, Endocrinology, and Nutrition Unit of Dr. Josep Trueta Hospital in Girona reported that a study of 127 elderly men who ate either a Mediterranean diet with nuts, a Mediterranean diet with olive oil, or a low-Fat diet revealed that after two years, both types of Mediterranean diet resulted in a significant improvement in bone health.

As you can see, the health benefits of the Mediterranean diet have been widely and comprehensively studied. Again and again, the Mediterranean diet is found to be an excellent way to improve heart, bone, and overall health and reduce the risk of cardiovascular disease, type 2 diabetes, metabolic syndrome, and some types of cancer.

The fact that it's a delicious way to eat that can also help you lose weight just makes the Mediterranean diet that much more appealing!

A Delicious Path to Weight Loss

One of the best ways to ensure that a diet will help you reach your weight-loss goals is to choose one that allows you to eat a wide variety of delicious foods and doesn't require you to go hungry, do without all of your favorite treats, or buy a lot of expensive and obscure ingredients. This is where the Mediterranean diet really stands out. There are no strict rules to follow, and there is no deprivation or any need to drive all over town hunting down exotic ingredients or expensive supplements.

DID YOU KNOW? Not only is the Mediterranean diet healthful and delicious, but it can also be a very low-cost way to lose weight. The emphasis on eating whole foods (rather than processed) in season and shopping at farmers' markets means that you'll be buying produce at its peak of flavor and at the lowest prices. As everyone knows, an apple is cheaper than a strawberry in November, and it tastes better, too!

How the Mediterranean Diet Can Help You Lose Weight

For some individuals who follow it, the Mediterranean eating regimen brings about weight reduction in a characteristic and easy manner.

While most weight reduction eats fewer Carbs center around counting Calories, following a severe menu, gauging and estimating food sources, or undertaking a thorough activity program, the Mediterranean eating routine spotlights on partaking in a wide assortment of energizing food sources and investing in some opportunity to relish suppers and offer them with others. It's a blissful approach to eating as well as a refreshing one.

By eliminating handled food sources and quick food sources from your eating regimen, which are loaded down with unhealthful Fats, sugar, and synthetic compounds, you can altogether diminish your caloric admission while really eating more food. Without counting Calories or Fat grams, you can exchange unhealthful, "void" food varieties for those that advance great wellbeing as well as help the deficiency of putting away Fat.

For quite a long time, the low-Fat eating regimen has been advanced as the genuine main method for getting in shape, yet we presently realize that this simply isn't accurate. Truth be told, a low-Fat eating routine all the time brings about weight gain and can be unhealthful for sure.

An examination emergency clinic in Switzerland as of late inspected six separate investigations contrasting the Mediterranean eating regimen and a low-Fat eating routine. Individuals who followed the Mediterranean eating regimen for the investigations experienced more noteworthy weight reduction, lower muscle versus Fat ratios, lower pulse, and preferable glucose levels over those on the low-Fat eating routine.

Since it incorporates such a wide assortment of fortifying, new food sources, the Mediterranean eating regimen supplies a restorative measure of fiber and "great" Fats, the two of which backing weight reduction by assisting you with feeling full. A high-fiber diet likewise eases back the rate at which sugar is retained into your circulatory system, which assists control both blood with sugaring and insulin levels. An excessive amount of insulin in the circulatory system stops Fat misfortune, as insulin triggers Fat capacity. Fiber from entire grains, natural products, and vegetables additionally assists with further developing processing, which can be a significant component in weight reduction. A large number of the cell reinforcements found in new products of the soil, like lutein in apples, have likewise been displayed to support weight reduction.

Generally speaking, the Mediterranean eating regimen permits individuals to get more fit normally and invigoratingly, without going hungry or killing nutritional categories. You'll not exclusively have the option to get thinner on the eating regimen; you'll live it up while you do.

Red meat and sweets
Infrequent consumption
(once/week)

Fish, seafood, white meat, eggs, yogurt and cheese
Regular consumption
(twice/week)

Fruit, vegetables, whole grain, olive oil, nuts, legumes, spices
Daily consumption

Chapter 2

The Pyramid of the Mediterranean Diet

The Med diet food pyramid is a nourishment manual for assisting individuals with eating the right food varieties in the right amounts and the recommended recurrence according to the conventional dietary patterns of individuals from the Mediterranean coast nations.

The pyramid was created by the World Health Organization, Harvard School of Public Health, and the former ways Preservation Trust in 1993.

There are 6 food layers in the pyramid with physical activity at the base, which is an important element to maintain a healthy life.

Just above it is the first food layer, consisting of whole grains, bread, beans, pasta, and nuts. It is the strongest layer having foods that are recommended by the Mediterranean diet. Next comes fruits and vegetables. As you move up the pyramid, you will find foods that must be eaten less and less, with the topmost layer consisting of foods that should be avoided or restricted.

The Mediterranean eating regimen food pyramid is straightforward. It gives a simple method for following the eating plan.

The Food Layers

Whole Grains, Bread, Beans – The lowest and the widest layer with foods that are strongly recommended. Your meals should be made of mostly these items. Eat whole-wheat bread, whole-wheat pita, whole-grain roll and bun, whole-grain cereal, whole-wheat pasta, and brown rice. 4 to 6 servings a day will give you plenty of nutrition.

Fruits, Vegetables – Almost as important as the lowest layer. Eat non-starchy vegetables daily like asparagus, broccoli, beets, tomatoes, carrots, cucumber, cabbage, cauliflower, turnips 4 to 8 servings daily. Take 2 to 4 servings of fruits every day. Choose seasonal fresh fruits.

Olive oil – Cook your meals preferably in extra-virgin olive oil. Daily consumption. Healthy for the body, it lowers the low-density lipoProtein cholesterol (LDL) and total cholesterol level. Up to 2 tablespoons of olive oil is allowed. The diet also allows canola oil.

Fish – Now, we come to the food layers that have to be consumed weekly and not daily. You can have fish 2 to 3 times a week. Best is Fatty sea fish like tuna, herring, salmon, and sardines. Sea fish will give you heart-healthy omega-3 Fatty acids and plenty of Proteins. Shellfish, including mussels, oysters, shrimp, and clams, are also good.

Poultry, cheese, yogurt – The diet should include cheese, yogurt, eggs, chicken, and other poultry products, but in moderation. Maximum 2-3 times in a week. Low-Fat dairy is best. Soy milk, cheese, or yogurt is better.

Meats, sweets – This is the topmost layer consisting of foods that are best avoided. You can have them once or twice in a month max. Remember, the Mediterranean diet is plant-based. There is very little room for meat, especially red meat. If you cannot live without it, then take red meat in small portions. Choose lean cuts. Have sweets only to celebrate. For instance, you can have a couple of sweets after following the diet for a month.

Recommended Foods

For example, most people living in the region eat a diet rich in whole grains, vegetables, fruits, nuts, seeds, fish, Fats, and legumes. It is not a restrictive diet like the many low-Fat eating plans. Actually, Fat is encouraged, but only from healthy sources, such as polyunsaturated Fat (omega-3 Fatty acids) that you will get from fish and monounsaturated Fat from olive oil.

It is strongly plant-based but not exclusively vegetarian. The diet recommends limiting the intake of saturated Fats and trans Fats that you get from red meat and processed foods. You must also limit the intake of dairy products.

Fruits and vegetables – Eat daily. Try to have 7-10 servings every day. Meals are strongly based on plant-based foods. Eat fresh fruits and vegetables. Pick from seasonal varieties.

Whole grains – Eat whole-grain cereal, bread, and pasta. All parts of whole grains – the germ, bran, and endosperm provide healthy nutrients. These nutrients are lost when the grain is refined into white flour.

Healthy Fats only – Avoid butter for cooking. Switch to olive oil. Dip your bread in flavored olive oil instead of applying margarine or butter on bread. Trans Fats and saturated Fats can cause heart disease.

Fish – Fish is encouraged. Eat Fatty fish like herring, mackerel, albacore tuna, sardines, lake trout, and salmon. Fatty fish will give you plenty of healthy omega-3 Fatty acids that reduce inflammations. Omega-3 Fatty acids also reduce blood clotting, decrease triglycerides, and improve heart health. Eat fresh seafood two times a week. Avoid deep-fried fish. Choose grilled fish.

Legumes – Provides the body with minerals, Protein, complex carbohydrates, polyunsaturated Fatty acids, and fiber. Eat daily.

Dairy and poultry – You can eat eggs, milk products, and chicken throughout the week, but in moderation. Restrict cheese. Go for plain or low-Fat Greek yogurt instead of cheese.

Nuts and seeds – 3 or more servings every week. Eat a variety of nuts, seeds, and beans. Walnuts and almonds are all allowed.

Red meat – The Mediterranean diet is not meat-based. You can still have red meat, but only once or twice a week max. If you love red meat, then make sure that it is lean. Take small portions only. Avoid processed meats like salami, sausage, and bologna.

Olive Oil – The key source of Fat. Olive oil will give you monounsaturated Fat that lowers the LDL or low-density lipoProtein cholesterol and total cholesterol level. Seeds and nuts will also provide you monounsaturated Fat. You can also have canola oil but no cream, butter, mayonnaise, or margarine. Take up to 4 tablespoons of olive oil a day. For best results, only take extra-virgin olive oil.

Wine – Red wine is allowed, but with moderation. Don't take more than a glass of red wine daily. Best take only 3-4 days a week.

Desserts – Say no to ice cream, sweets, pies, and chocolate cake. Fresh fruits are good.

Main Components

- Focus on natural foods – Avoid processed foods as much as you can

- Be flexible – Plan to have a variety of foods

- Consume fruits, vegetables, healthy Fats, and whole grains daily

- Have weekly plans for poultry, fish, eggs, and beans

- Take dairy products moderately

- Limit red meat intake

- Take water instead of soda. Only take wine when you are having a meal.

Foods in the Traditional Mediterranean Diet

Whole Grains	Vege-tables	Fruits	Protein	Dairy	Others
Brown rice	Arti-chokes	Apples	Almonds	Low/non-Fat plain or Greek yogurt	Bay leaf
Oats	Arugula	Apricots	Walnuts		Basil
Bulgur	Beats	Avocados	Pistachios		Olive oil
Barley	Broccoli	Figs	Cannellini Beans	Manche-go cheese	Red wine
Farrow	Cucum-bers	Olives	Chickpeas	Brie che-ese	Mint
Wheat berries	Eggplant	Strawber-ries	Kidney beans	Ricotta cheese	Pepper
Pasta	Onions	Tomatoes	Salmon	Parmesan cheese	Cumin
Whole grain bread	Spinach	Melons	Tuna	Feta che-ese	Garlic
Couscous	Potatoes	Grapes	Eggs		Anise spice

Foods Allowed

You should consume plenty of fruits, nuts, vegetables, seeds, beans, whole grains, herbs, and legumes. Olive oil and canola oil are both allowed.

Eat Moderately

Fish, seafood, chicken, eggs, low-Fat cheese, and yogurt.

Restricted Foods

This list includes refined grains like white rice, white bread, sweets, baked products, and soda. Also, restrict processed meats and red meat. Watch out for high-Fat dairy products like butter and ice cream and trans-Fats in margarine and processed foods.

Food Groups and Daily/ Weekly Servings	Serving Sizes
Non-starchy vegetables 4 to 8 servings	1 serving is ½ cup of cooked vegetables or 1 cup of raw vegetables Asparagus, artichoke, broccoli, beets, Brussels sprouts, cabbage, celery, cauliflower, carrots, eggplant, tomatoes, cucumber, onion, zucchini, turnips, mushrooms, and salad greens. Note: Peas, corn, and potatoes are starchy vegetables.
Fruits 2 to 4 servings	One serving is a small fruit or ½ cup juice or ¼ cup dried fruit. Eat fresh fruits for their nutrients and fiber. You can also have canned fruits with their juice and frozen fruits without added sugar.
Legumes, Nuts, Seeds 2 to 4 servings	Legumes – 1 serving is ½ cup cooked kidney, pinto, garbanzo, soy, navy beans, lentils, or split peas, or ¼ cup Fat-free beans. Nuts and Seeds – 1 serving is 2 tablespoons of sesame or sunflower seeds, 1 tablespoon peanut butter, 7-8 pecans or walnuts, 12-15 almonds, 20 peanuts. Take 1-2 servings of nuts or seeds and 1-2 servings of legumes. Legumes will give you minerals, fiber, and Protein; whole nuts provide unsaturated Fat without increasing your LDL cholesterol levels.

Low-Fat Dairy 2 to 3 servings	1 serving is 1 cup of skim milk, nonFat yogurt, or 1 oz. low-Fat cheese Replace dairy products with soy yogurt, calcium-rich soy milk, or soy cheese. You need a vitamin D and calcium supplement if you are taking less than 2 servings daily.
Fish 2 to 3 times a week	One serving is 3 ounces Bake, sauté, roast, broil, poach, or grill. It is best to eat Fatty fish, such as sardines, herring, salmon, or mackerel. Fish will provide you omega-3 Fats, which offers many health benefits.
Poultry 1 to 3 times a week	One serving is 3 ounces Sautè, bake, grill, or stir fry the poultry. Eat without the skin.
Whole grains, starchy vegetables 4 to 6 servings	One serving is 1 ounce of – ½ cup sweet potatoes, potatoes, corn, or peas 1 slice of whole-wheat bread 1 small whole-grain roll ½ large whole-grain bun 6 whole-grain crackers 6-inch whole wheat pita ½ cup cooked brown rice, whole-wheat pasta, or barley ½ cup whole-grain cereal (cracked wheat, oatmeal, quinoa) Whole grains provide fiber and keep the stomach full, promoting weight loss.

Healthy Fats 4 to 6 servings	One serving is – 1 tablespoon of regular salad dressing 2 tablespoons of light salad dressing 2 teaspoons light margarine 1 teaspoon canola or olive oil 1 teaspoon regular mayonnaise 1/8 avocado 5 olives These are mostly unsaturated Fats, so your LDL cholesterol levels won't increase. Men – Max 2 drinks a day. Women – Max 1 drink a day.
Alcohol	1 drink = 4 ounces of wine, 12-ounce beer, or 1-1/2-ounces liquor (vodka, whiskey, brandy, etc.). Avoid alcohol if you have high triglycerides or high BP.

The Med Lifestyle

Not just the food, but the correct lifestyle is also equally important. This includes both getting adequate exercise and making social connections.

Physical Activity – It is at the base of the food pyramid, even lower than the first and most important food layer – getting adequate physical activity is essential. This includes exercising regularly, swimming, biking, running, and playing an active sport. However, there are other ways as well to maintain good health.

You will find many from the Mediterranean region not going to the gym. But, they are not inactive. Many are into a lot of manual labor. They will walk to their workplace, to the bakery, or the farmer's market. They walk to their friend's home. Even a daily walk and moderate exercise will help. Natural movements are good. Avoid the escalator. Take the stairs instead.

How much exercise is good? Working out is always good for health. You don't have to lift weights, though. 10-15 minutes on the treadmill and gym bike 5 days a week should be good. Half an hour of moderate-intensity activity will do. It is better if you can also do a few muscle-strengthening activities twice a week. You can likewise take a stab at strolling 200 minutes every week or, in any event, cultivating for an hour 4-5 times each week.

Cook at Home - Home-prepared food is generally more grounded than eating out. For instance, eatery-cooked pasta will have higher segments of sodium.

Again, you can have one portion of whole-grain spaghetti with tomato sauce and spinach instead of the heavy cream sauce. You can control the ingredients by preparing the meals at home. Home-cooked meals have lots of minerals, vitamins, and fiber and are lower in added sugar, sodium, and saturated Fat.

Eat Together – Mealtime should be a social experience. Eating together with friends or family is a great stress buster. It will boost your mood, which will positively impact your physical health. Plus, it will prevent you from overeating too. You will often find the Mediterranean people eating together in a garden.

Switch the TV off and enjoy your meal. Monitor what the kids are eating. If you live alone, invite a co-worker, neighbor, or friend. You can even invite someone and prepare meals together.

Laugh Often – Have you heard of the popular saying, "Laughter is the best medicine"? This is true in the Mediterranean culture. Many are individuals with big personalities. Their conversations are full of humor. They love to tell stories. Enjoy life and keep a positive attitude/

Live a Simple Life – Consider food, for example. You won't find them buying too much of anything. The idea of buying any ingredient in bulk is foreign to them. They buy fresh, focusing on daily needs. And of course, fresh food is always best.

Enjoy Every Bite – Slow down and enjoy each bite. Many will eat for survival. But in the Mediterranean belt, they love their food. They enjoy it. Don't eat on the go. Sit down and have a proper meal.

Health Benefits of the Med Diet

Heart disease and stroke – The Mediterranean diet recommends limited eating of processed foods, red meat, and refined bread, which contributes towards a lower risk of heart ailments and stroke. A study carried out over 12 years among 25,000 women found that women eating this diet were able to reduce their risk of heart disease by 25%.

The PREDIMED (1) study was carried out amongst men and women with a high risk of cardiovascular disease and type-2 diabetes in Spain. After 5 years of research, it was discovered that those who had a calorie-unrestricted Mediterranean diet had a 30% lower risk of heart issues.

Alzheimer's – Research also suggests that the diet can improve blood sugar levels, cholesterol, and blood vessel health, which in turn may lower the risk of dementia and Alzheimer's disease. A 2018 study (2) scanned the brains of 70 people for dementia and monitored their food habits. After 2 years, it was observed that those on the Mediterranean diet had fewer Protein plaques of beta-amyloid deposits than others, and thus a lower risk of Alzheimer's.

Other studies have also revealed that the Mediterranean diet may also prevent the decline of thinking skills and memory with age as there is an increased supply of oxygen and nutrients to the brain.

The diet is packed with antioxidants, such as olive oil and nuts, which may delay mental decline. A link between consuming fish and a lower risk of Alzheimer's has also been found.

Diabetes – The diet with healthy Carbs and whole grains offers big benefits like stabilizing the blood sugar level. Complex whole-grain Carbs like wheat berries, buckwheat, and quinoa improve overall energy and keep the sugar level even in your blood. Research on more than 400 people between the age of 55 and 80 years have revealed that the Mediterranean diet can lower (3) the risk of type-2 diabetes by 52%. This study was carried out over 4 years.

Parkinson's disease – The diet is rich in antioxidants, which may prevent oxidative stress or cell damage, thus reducing the risk of Parkinson's disease by as much as 50%.

Weight loss – The Mediterranean eating regimen gives you a lot of fiber that will cause you to feel satisfied. You will not indulge, therefore. The eating routine further develops digestion and advances sound weight reduction. Make sure to zero in on consuming sinewy vegetables, organic products, beans, and vegetables rather than straightforward starches. This is a protected and reasonable method for getting in shape as barely anything is denied in the general supper plan. The U.S. News & World Report ranked the Mediterranean diet n.1 in the 'Best Overall Diet' category for 2019.

Cancer – The diet has also been linked to a lower risk of certain types of cancer. Researchers looked at the findings of 83 studies covering more than 2 million people and concluded that it may reduce (4) the risk of breast, gastric, colorectal, and colon cancer. The cancer mortality rate is significantly lower amongst those who eat this diet. This has been attributed to the higher intake of whole grains, vegetables, and fruits. The result of this study was published in the Nutrients journal.

Another study according to the JAMA Internal Medicine journal discovered that women eating this diet were able to reduce the risk of breast cancer by 62%.

Inflammation – Fatty fish like tuna, mackerel, and salmon have a lot of omega-3 Fatty acids that can reduce inflammation. Besides, omega-3 will also improve the elasticity of your skin and make it stronger.

Rheumatoid arthritis – In this autoimmune disease, the body's immune system attacks the joints by mistake, causing swelling and pain. The National Institutes of Health's Office of Dietary Supplements has suggested that long-chain omega-3 Fatty acids, which you will find in Fatty fish, provide relief from the symptoms of RA or Rheumatoid arthritis.

Good for the gut – The Med diet provides 7% more good bacteria in the microbiome compared to those eating a traditional western diet as it is a plant-based eating plan with a lot of fruits, vegetables, seeds, nuts, and legumes. This improves gut health.

Several other scientific studies have also revealed the health gains of eating this diet.

The Rockefeller Foundation – This was one of the first studies on the diet carried out on the Greek island of Crete. The Greek government asked for help from the Rockefeller Foundation after World War II because the island was severely destroyed after the war, and the people were in abject poverty. Many field staff were sent, including nutritionists and nurses.

They visited many homes and took notes on their food and drinking habits. To their surprise, it was found that most people were in good health and were living into old age in spite of the poverty. Very few people were suffering from heart disease, though 40% of their Calories were coming from Fat.

Ancel Keys' 7 Country Study – This was a follow-up study to find out the heart health condition of residents around the Mediterranean Sea. It was carried out in the late 1950s by Ancel Keys, an American scientist. In the late 1950s, 92 out of 1000 men in the United States were suffering from heart diseases. But in Crete, Ancel found to his surprise, that only 3 men out of 1000 had heart conditions.

The University of Barcelona Study – In recent times, the University of Barcelona

Carried out a study on 7000 men and women over 5 years. They found that there were significant improvements in heart health when the participants ate a Mediterranean diet. The risk of cardiovascular disease dropped by almost 30%. And they were also high-risk individuals, as the participants were all overweight people and also diabetics and smokers. The results of this 2013 study were published by the New England Journal of Medicine.

The Cochrane Study – Carried out in the same year, this study too arrived at the same conclusion. The researchers concluded by noting that a high-Protein, high-fiber, low-glycemic index, low-carbohydrate diet improves cardiovascular health and reduces the risk of diabetes.

Hundreds of studies have been carried out in recent years to verify whether the diet improves health or not. Almost all of them have concluded that those who eat a Mediterranean diet have lower risks of Alzheimer's, dementia, and diabetes. Many other health advantages have also been noted.

Chapter 3

Mediterranean Egg Recipes

Breakfast Egg on Avocado

Preparation:
10'

Cooking:
15'

Servings:
6

NUTRITION

Calories: 252
Carbs: 4.0 gr.
Protein: 14.0 gr.
Fat: 20.0 gr.

INGREDIENTS

- 6 medium eggs
- 1/2 tsp sea salt
- 1/4 tsp black pepper
- 1 tsp garlic powder
- 1/4 cup Parmesan cheese (grated or shredded)

- 3 medium avocados (cut in half, pitted, skin on)

DIRECTIONS:

1. Get ready biscuit tins and preheat the broiler to 350oF.
2. To guarantee that the egg will fit inside the pit of the avocado, gently scratch off 1/3 of the meat.
3. Put the avocado on a biscuit tin to guarantee that it faces with the top-up.
4. Uniformly season every avocado with pepper, salt, and garlic powder.
5. Add one egg on every avocado pit and top tops with cheddar.
6. Pop in the broiler and prepare until the egg white is set, around 15 minutes.
7. Serve and appreciate.

Breakfast Egg-artichoke Casserole

Preparation:
10'

Cooking:
35'

Servings:
8

NUTRITION
Calories: 302
Carbs: 10.8 gr.
Protein: 22.6 gr.
Fat: 18.7 gr.

INGREDIENTS

- 16 large eggs
- 10-ounce box frozen chopped spinach, thawed and drained well
- 14 ounce can artichoke hearts, drained
- 1 garlic clove, minced
- 1 cup shredded white cheddar
- 1 teaspoon salt

- 1/2 cup ricotta cheese
- 1/2 cup parmesan cheese
- 1/2 teaspoon dried thyme
- 1/2 teaspoon crushed red pepper
- 1/4 cup milk
- 1/4 cup shaved onion

DIRECTIONS:

1. Delicately oil a 9x13-inch baking dish and preheat the broiler to 350oF.
2. In a huge blending bowl, add eggs and milk. Blend completely.
3. With a paper towel, press out the overabundance dampness from the spinach leaves and add to the bowl of eggs.
4. Into little pieces, break the artichoke hearts and separate the leaves. Add to the bowl of eggs.
5. Aside from the ricotta cheddar, add remaining fixings in the bowl of eggs and blend completely.
6. Empty egg combination into the pre-arranged dish.
7. Equitably add bits of ricotta cheddar on top of the eggs and afterward pop in the broiler.
8. Heat until eggs are set and don't shake when shook, around 35 minutes.
9. Remove from the oven and evenly divide into suggested servings. Enjoy.

Eggs, Mint, and Tomatoes

Preparation:
10'

Cooking:
15'

Servings:
2

NUTRITION
Calories: 300
Carbs: 17.7 gr.
Protein: 11 gr.
Fat: 15.3 gr.

INGREDIENTS

- eggs, whisked
- tomatoes, cubed
- 2 teaspoons olive oil
- 1 tablespoon mint, chopped
- 1 tablespoon chives, chopped
- Salt and black pepper to the taste

DIRECTIONS:

1. Heat up a pan with the oil over medium heat, add the tomatoes and the rest of the ingredients except the eggs, stir and cook for 5 minutes.
2. Add the eggs, toss, cook for 10 minutes more, divide between plates and serve.

Brekky Egg-potato Hash

Preparation:
10'

Cooking:
25'

Servings:
2

NUTRITION
Calories: 190
Carbs: 2.9 gr.
Protein: 11.7 gr.
Fat: 12.3 gr.

INGREDIENTS

- 1 zucchini, diced
- 1/2 cup chicken broth
- ½ pound cooked chicken
- 1 tablespoon olive oil
- 4 ounces shrimp
- Salt and ground black pepper to taste
- 1 large sweet potato, diced
- 2 eggs
- 1/4 teaspoon cayenne pepper
- 2 teaspoons garlic powder
- 1 cup fresh spinach (optional)

DIRECTIONS:

1. In a skillet, add olive oil.
2. Fry the shrimp, cooked chicken, and sweet potato for 2 minutes.
3. Add the cayenne pepper, garlic powder, and salt, and toss for 4 minutes.
4. Add the zucchini and toss for another 3 minutes.
5. Whisk the eggs in a bowl and add to the skillet.
6. Season using salt and pepper. Cover with the lid.
7. Cook for 1 minute and add the chicken broth.
8. Cover and cook for another 8 minutes on high heat.
9. Add the spinach and toss for 2 more minutes.
10. Serve immediately.

Dill and Tomato Frittata

Preparation:
10'

Cooking:
35'

Servings:
6

NUTRITION
Calories: 149
Carbs: 9.93 gr.
Protein: 13.26 gr.
Fat: 10.28 gr.

INGREDIENTS

- Pepper and salt to taste
- 1 tsp red pepper flakes
- 2 garlic cloves, minced
- ½ cup crumbled goat cheese – optional
- 2 tbsp fresh chives, chopped

- 2 tbsp fresh dill, chopped
- 4 tomatoes, diced
- 8 eggs, whisked
- 1 tsp coconut oil

DIRECTIONS:

1. Grease a 9-inch round baking pan and preheat the oven to 325oF.
2. In a large bowl, mix well all ingredients and pour into prepped pan.
3. Pop into the oven and bake until middle is cooked through around 30-35 minutes.
4. Remove from oven and garnish with more chives and dill.

Breakfast Taco Scramble

Preparation:
15'

Cooking:
1 h 25'

Servings:
4

NUTRITION
Calories: 450
Carbs: 24.5 gr.
Protein: 46 gr.
Fat: 19 gr.

INGREDIENTS

- 8 large eggs, beaten
- 1/4 tsp seasoning salt
- 2 tbsp Greek seasoning
- 1 lb. 99% lean ground turkey
- 1/4 cup water
- 1/2 small onion, minced
- 2 tbsp bell pepper, minced
- 4 oz. can tomato sauce

- 1/4 cup chopped scallions or cilantro for topping

For the potatoes:
- 12 (1 lb.) baby gold or red potatoes, quartered
- 4 tsp olive oil
- 3/4 tsp salt
- 1/2 tsp garlic powder
- fresh black pepper, to taste

DIRECTIONS:

1. In a large bowl, beat the eggs, season with seasoning salt. Preheat the oven to 425 degrees F. Spray a 9x12 or large oval casserole dish with cooking oil.
2. Add the potatoes 1 tbsp oil, 3/4 teaspoon salt, garlic powder, and black pepper and toss to coat. Bake for 45 minutes to 1 hour, tossing every 15 minutes.
3. In the meantime, brown the turkey in a large skillet over medium heat, breaking it up while it cooks. Once no longer pink, add in the Greek seasoning.
4. Add in the bell pepper, onion, tomato sauce, and water, stir and cover, simmer on low for about 20 minutes. Spray a different skillet with nonstick spray over medium heat.
5. Once heated, add in the eggs seasoned with 1/4 tsp of salt and scramble for 2–3 minutes, or cook until it sets.
6. Distribute 3/4 cup turkey and 2/3 cup eggs, divide the potatoes in each storage container, and store for 3-4 days.

Smoked Salmon and Poached Eggs on Toast

Preparation:
10'

Cooking:
4

Servings:
-

NUTRITION
Calories: 459.4
Carbs: 33.2 gr.
Protein: 31.1 gr.
Fat: 21.9 gr.

INGREDIENTS

- 2 oz avocado smashed
- 2 slices of bread toasted
- Pinch of kosher salt and cracked black pepper
- 1/4 tsp freshly squeezed lemon juice
- 2 eggs see notes, poached

- 3.5 oz smoked salmon
- 1 TBSP. thinly sliced scallions
- Splash of Kikkoman soy sauce optional
- Microgreens are optional

DIRECTIONS:

1. Take a small bowl and then smash the avocado into it. Then, add the lemon juice and a pinch of salt into the mixture. Then, mix it well and set it aside.
2. After that, poach the eggs and toast the bread for some time.
3. Once the bread is toasted, you will have to spread the avocado on both slices and add the smoked salmon to each slice.
4. Thereafter, carefully transfer the poached eggs to the respective toasts.
5. Add a splash of Kikkoman soy sauce and some cracked pepper; then, just garnish with scallions and microgreens.

Low-Carb Baked Eggs with Avocado and Feta

Preparation:
10'

Cooking:
15'

Servings:
2

NUTRITION
Calories: 280 kcal
Carbs: 9.3 gr.
Protein: 11.3 gr.
Fat: 23.5 gr.

INGREDIENTS

- 1 avocado
- 4 eggs
- 2-3 tbsp. crumbled feta cheese
- Nonstick cooking spray
- Pepper and salt to taste

DIRECTIONS:

1. In the first place, you should preheat the broiler to 400 degrees F.
2. From that point onward, when the broiler is at the appropriate temperature, you should put the gratin dishes right on the baking sheet.
3. Then, at that point, warm the dishes on the stove for right around 10 minutes.
4. After that cycle, you want to break the eggs into individual ramekins.
5. Then, at that point, let the avocado and eggs come to room temperature for no less than 10 minutes.
6. Then, at that point, strip the avocado appropriately and cut it every half into 6-8 cuts.
7. You should remove the dishes from the stove and shower them with a nonstick splash.
8. Then, you ought to organize all of the cut avocados in the dishes and tip two eggs into each dish.
9. Sprinkle with feta, add pepper and salt to taste
10. Last, heat it for 12-15 minutes or until egg whites are set, and the egg yolks are done as you would prefer. Serve hot.

Pastry-Less Spanakopita

Preparation:
5'

Cooking:
20'

Servings:
4

NUTRITION
Calories: 325
Carbs: 7.3 gr.
Protein: 11.2 gr.
Fat: 27.9 gr.

INGREDIENTS

- 1/3 cup of Extra virgin olive oil
- 1/8 teaspoons black pepper, add as per taste
- 4 lightly beaten eggs
- 1/8 teaspoon of Sea salt, add to taste
- 7 cups of lettuce, preferably a spring mix (mesclun)
- 1/2 cup of crumbled Feta cheese
- 1 finely chopped medium yellow onion

DIRECTIONS:

1. For this delicious recipe, you need to first start by preheating the oven to 180C and grease the flan dish.
2. Once done, pour the additional virgin olive oil into a huge pot and hotness it over medium hotness with the onions until they are clear. To that, add greens and continue to mix until every one of the fixings are withered.
3. In the wake of finishing that, you ought to prepare it with salt and pepper and move the greens to the pre-arranged dish and sprinkle on some feta .
4. Pour the eggs and bake them for 20 minutes till it is cooked through and slightly brown.

Chapter 4

Mediterranean Breakfast Recipes

Banana-Coconut Breakfast

Preparation:
10'

Cooking:
3'

Servings:
4

NUTRITION
Calories: 279
Carbs: 25.46 gr.
Protein: 6.4 gr.
Fiber: 5.9 gr.

INGREDIENTS

- 1 ripe banana
- 1 cup desiccated coconut
- 1 cup coconut milk
- 3 tablespoons raisins, chopped
- 2 tablespoon ground flax seed
- 1 teaspoon vanilla
- A dash of cinnamon
- A dash of nutmeg
- Salt to taste

DIRECTIONS:

1. Place all ingredients in a deep pan.
2. Allow simmering for 3 minutes on low heat.
3. Place in individual containers.
4. Put a label and store it in the fridge.
5. Allow thawing at room temperature before heating in the microwave oven.

Chocolate Banana Smoothie

Preparation:
5'

Cooking:
0'

Servings:
2

NUTRITION

Calories: 219

Carbs: 57gr.

Fat: 2gr.

INGREDIENTS

- 1 banana, peeled
- 1 cup unsweetened almond milk, or skim milk
- 1 cup crushed ice
- 3 tablespoons unsweetened cocoa powder
- 3 tablespoons honey

DIRECTIONS:

1. Combine the bananas, ice, almond milk, cocoa powder, and honey in a blender. Blend until smooth.

Raspberry Vanilla Smoothie

Preparation:
5'

Cooking:
5'

Servings:
2

NUTRITION
Calories: 155
Carbs: 30 gr.
Fat: 2 gr.

INGREDIENTS

- 1 cup frozen raspberries
- 6-ounce container of vanilla Greek yogurt
- ½ cup of unsweetened vanilla al mond milk

DIRECTIONS:

1. Take all of your ingredients and place them in a blender. Process until smooth and liquified.

Blueberry Banana Protein Smoothie

Preparation:
5'

Cooking:
5'

Servings:
1

NUTRITION
Calories: 230
Carbs: 32.9 gr.
Fat: 2.6 gr.

INGREDIENTS

- ½ cup frozen and unsweetened blueberries
- ½ banana slices up
- ¾ cup plain non Fat Greek yogurt
- ¾ cup unsweetened vanilla almond milk
- 2 cups of ice cubes

DIRECTIONS:

1. Add all of the ingredients into a blender. Blend until smooth.

Quinoa Fruit Salad

Preparation:
5'

Cooking:
20'

Servings:
4

NUTRITION

Calories: 308

Carbs: 34 gr.

Protein: 4.4 gr.

Fat: 18.2 gr.

INGREDIENTS

For the Quinoa:
- 1 cup quinoa
- 2 cups water
- Pinch of salt
- 3 tablespoons honey

For the Honey Lime Dressing:
- 2 tablespoons finely chopped fresh mint
- Juice of 1 large lime

For the fruit:
- 1 1/2 cups blueberries
- 1 1/2 cups sliced strawberries
- 1 1/2 cups chopped mango
- Extra chopped mint for garnish-optional

DIRECTIONS:

1. Using a sifter, flush the quinoa under cool water. Add quinoa, water, and salt to a medium pot and heat to the point of boiling over medium heat. Boil for 5 minutes.
2. Turn the heat to low and stew for around 15 minutes or until water is retained. Remove from heat and fluff with a fork. Let quinoa cool to room temperature.
3. To make the Honey Lime Dressing: In a medium bowl, whisk the lime squeeze, honey, and mint together until consolidated. Consolidate quinoa, blueberries, strawberries, and mango in a huge bowl. Pour honey lime dressing over the natural product salad and blend until all-around joined.
4. Garnish with additional mint, if desired. Serve at room temperature or chilled.

Note: Use your favorite fruit in this salad. Blackberries, kiwi, peaches, raspberries, grapes, pineapple, etc., are great options!

Paleo Almond Banana Pancakes

Preparation:
10'

Cooking:
10'

Servings:
3

NUTRITION
Calories: 306
Carbs: 3.6 gr.
Protein: 14.4 gr.
Fat: 26.0 gr.

INGREDIENTS

- ¼ cup almond flour
- ½ teaspoon ground cinnamon
- 3 eggs
- 1 banana, mashed
- 1 tablespoon almond butter
- 1 teaspoon vanilla extract
- 1 teaspoon olive oil
- Sliced banana to serve

DIRECTIONS:

1. Whisk the eggs in a mixing bowl until they become fluffy.
2. In another bowl, mash the banana using a fork and add to the egg mixture.
3. Add the vanilla, almond butter, cinnamon, and almond flour.
4. Mix into a smooth batter.
5. Heat the olive oil in a skillet.
6. Add one spoonful of the batter and fry them on both sides.
7. Keep doing these steps until you are done with all the batter.
8. Add some sliced banana on top before serving.

Mediterranean Breakfast Salad

Preparation:
10'

Cooking:
20'

Servings:
4

NUTRITION
Carbs: 6.71 gr.
Protein 3.4 gr.
Fat 3.46 gr.

INGREDIENTS

- 4 whole eggs
- 2 cups of cherry tomatoes or heirloom tomatoes cut in half or wedges
- 10 cups of arugula
- A 1/2 chopped seedless cucumber
- 1 large avocado
- 1 cup cooked or cooled quinoa

- 1/2 cup of chopped mixed herbs like dill and mint
- 1 cup of chopped Almonds
- 1 lemon
- Extra virgin olive oil
- Sea salt
- Freshly ground black pepper

DIRECTIONS:

1. In this recipe, the eggs are the first thing that needs to be cooked. Start with soft boiling the eggs. To do that, you need to get water in a pan and let it sit to boil. Once it starts boiling, reduce the heat to simmer and lower the eggs into the water and let them cook for about 7 minutes. After they are boiled, wash the eggs with cold water and set them aside. Peel them when they are cool and ready to use.
2. Combine quinoa, arugula, cucumbers, and tomatoes in a bowl and add a little bit of olive oil over the top. Toss it with salt and pepper to equally season all of it.
3. Once all that is done, serve the salad on four plates and garnish it with sliced avocados and the halved eggs. After that, season it with some more pepper and salt.
4. To top it all off, use almonds and sprinkle some herbs and some lemon zest and olive oil.

Greek Beans Tortillas

Preparation:
5'

Cooking:
20'

Servings:
4

INGREDIENTS

- 1 red onion, chopped
- 2 garlic cloves, minced
- 1 tablespoon olive oil
- 1 green bell pepper, sliced
- 3 cups canned pinto beans, drained, and rinsed
- 2 red chili peppers, chopped
- 4 tablespoon parsley, chopped
- 1 teaspoon cumin, ground
- A pinch of salt and black pepper
- 4 whole wheat Greek tortillas
- 1 cup cheddar cheese, shredded

NUTRITION

Calories: 673
Carbs: 75.4 gr.
Protein: 39 gr.
Fat: 14.9 gr.

DIRECTIONS:

1. Heat up a dish with the oil over medium hotness, add the onion and sauté for 5 minutes.
2. Add the other fixings except for the tortillas and the cheddar, mix, and cook for 15 minutes.
3. Spread the mustard on each bread cut, partition the bacon and the other fixings on one cut, top with the other one, cut down the middle, and serve for breakfast.
4. Divide the beans mix on each Greek tortilla, also divide the cheese, roll the tortillas, and serve for breakfast.

Baked Cauliflower Hash

Preparation:
10'

Cooking:
25'

Servings:
4

NUTRITION
Calories: 367
Carbs: 16.8 gr.
Protein 12.2 gr.
Fat: 14.3 gr.

INGREDIENTS

- 4 cups cauliflower florets
- 1 tablespoon olive oil
- 2 cups white mushrooms, sliced
- 1 cup cherry tomatoes, halved
- 1 yellow onion, chopped
- 2 garlic cloves, minced

- ¼ teaspoon garlic powder
- 3 tablespoons basil, chopped
- 3 tablespoons mint, chopped
- 1 tablespoon dill, chopped

DIRECTIONS:

1. Heat up a dish with the oil over medium hotness, add the onion and sauté for 5 minutes.
2. Add the other fixings except for the tortillas and the cheddar, mix, and cook for 15 minutes.
3. Spread the mustard on each bread cut, partition the bacon and the other fixings on one cut, top with the other one, cut down the middle, and serve for breakfast.
4. Divide the beans mix on each Greek tortilla, also divide the cheese, roll the tortillas, and serve for breakfast.

Honey Almond Ricotta Spread with Peaches

Preparation:
5'

Cooking:
8'

Servings:
5

NUTRITION
Calories: 187kcal
Carbs: 19 gr.
Protein: 7gr.
Fat: 9gr.

INGREDIENTS

- 1/2 cup Fisher Sliced Almonds
- 1 cup whole milk ricotta
- 1/4 teaspoon almond extract
- Zest from an orange, optional
- 1 teaspoon honey
- Hearty whole-grain toast
- English muffin or bagel
- Extra Fisher sliced almonds
- Sliced peaches
- Extra honey for drizzling

DIRECTIONS:

1. Cut peaches into a proper shape and then brush them with olive oil. After that, set it aside.
2. Take a bowl; combine the ingredients for the filling. Set aside.
3. Then just preheat the grill to medium.
4. Place peaches cut side down onto the greased grill.
5. Close lid cover and then just grill until the peaches have softened, approximately 6-10 minutes, depending on the size of the peaches.
6. Then you will have to place peach halves onto a serving plate.
7. Put a spoon of about 1 tablespoon of ricotta mixture into the cavity (you are also allowed to use a small scooper).
8. Sprinkle it with slivered almonds, crushed amaretti cookies, and honey.
9. Decorate with the mint leaves.

Bacon, Spinach and Tomato Sandwich

Preparation:
5'

Cooking:
0'

Servings:
1

NUTRITION
Calories: 246
Fat: 11.2 gr.
Carbs: 17.5 gr.
Protein: 8.3 gr.

INGREDIENTS

- 2 whole-wheat bread slices, toasted
- 1 tablespoon Dijon mustard
- 3 bacon slices
- Salt and black pepper to the taste
- 2 tomato slices
- ¼ cup baby spinach

DIRECTIONS:

1. Spread the mustard on each bread slice, divide the bacon and the rest of the ingredients on one slice, top with the other one, cut in half, and serve for breakfast.

Cinnamon Apple and Lentils Porridge

Preparation:
5'

Cooking:
10'

Servings:
4

NUTRITION

Calories: 150

Fat: 2 gr.

Carbs: 3 gr.

Protein: 5 gr.

INGREDIENTS

- ½ cup walnuts, chopped
- 2 green apples, cored, peeled, and cubed
- 3 tablespoons maple syrup
- 3 cups almond milk
- ½ cup red lentils
- ½ teaspoon cinnamon powder
- ½ cup cranberries, dried
- 1 teaspoon vanilla extract

DIRECTIONS:

1. Put the milk in a pot, heat it up over medium heat, add the walnuts, apples, maple syrup, and the rest of the ingredients, toss, simmer for 10 minutes, divide into bowls and serve.

Seeds and Lentils Oats

Preparation:
10'

Cooking:
50'

Servings:
4

NUTRITION
Calories: 204
Fat: 7.1 gr.
Carbs: 27.6 gr.
Protein: 9.5 gr.

INGREDIENTS

- ½ cup red lentils
- ¼ cup pumpkin seeds, toasted
- 2 teaspoons olive oil
- ¼ cup rolled oats
- ¼ cup coconut flesh, shredded
- 1 tablespoon honey
- 1 tablespoon orange zest, grated
- 1 cup Greek yogurt
- 1 cup blackberries

DIRECTIONS:

1. Spread the lentils on a baking sheet lined with parchment paper, place them in the oven, and roast at 370 degrees F for 30 minutes.
2. Add the rest of the ingredients except the yogurt and the berries, toss and bake at 370 degrees F for 20 minutes more.
3. Transfer this to a bowl, add the rest of the ingredients, toss, divide into smaller bowls and serve for breakfast.

Walnuts Yogurt Mix

Preparation:
10'

Cooking:
0'

Servings:
6

NUTRITION
Calories: 388
Fat: 24.6 gr.
Carbs: 39.1 gr.
Protein: 10.2 gr.

INGREDIENTS

- 2 and ½ cups Greek yogurt
- 1 and ½ cups walnuts, chopped
- 1 teaspoon vanilla extract
- ¾ cup honey
- 2 teaspoons cinnamon powder

DIRECTIONS:

1. In a bowl, combine the yogurt with the walnuts and the rest of the ingredients, toss, divide into smaller bowls and keep in the fridge for 10 minutes before serving for breakfast.

Stuffed Pita Breads

Preparation:
5'

Cooking:
15'

Servings:
4

NUTRITION

Calories: 382

Fat: 1.8 gr.

Carbs: 66 gr.

Protein: 28.5 gr.

INGREDIENTS

- 1 and ½ tablespoons olive oil
- 1 tomato, cubed
- 1 garlic clove, minced
- 1 red onion, chopped
- ¼ cup parsley, chopped
- 15 ounces canned fava beans, drained and rinsed
- ¼ cup lemon juice
- Salt and dark pepper to the taste
- 4 entire wheat pita bread pockets

DIRECTIONS:

1. Heat up a dish with the oil over medium hotness, add the onion, mix, and sauté for 5 minutes.
2. Add the other fixings, mix, and cook for 10 minutes more Stuff the pita pockets with this blend and serve for breakfast.

Farro Salad

Preparation:
5'

Cooking:
4'

Servings:
2

NUTRITION
Calories 157
Fat: 13.7 gr.
Carbs: 8.6 gr.
Protein: 3.6 gr.

INGREDIENTS

- 1 tablespoon olive oil
- A pinch of salt and black pepper
- 1 bunch baby spinach, chopped
- 1 avocado, pitted, peeled, and chopped
- 1 garlic clove, minced
- 2 cups farro, already cooked
- ½ cup cherry tomatoes, cubed

DIRECTIONS:

1. Heat up a pan with the oil over medium heat, add the spinach, and the rest of the ingredients, toss, cook for 4 minutes, divide into bowls, and serve.

Cranberry and Dates Squares

Preparation:
30'

Cooking:
0'

Servings:
10

NUTRITION
Calories: 263
Fat: 13.4 gr.
Carbs: 14.3 gr.
Protein: 3.5 gr.

INGREDIENTS

- 12 dates, pitted and chopped
- 1 teaspoon vanilla extract
- ¼ cup honey
- ½ cup rolled oats
- ¾ cup cranberries, dried
- ¼ cup almond avocado oil, melted
- 1 cup walnuts, toasted, and chopped
- ¼ cup pumpkin seeds

DIRECTIONS:

1. In a bowl, mix the dates with the vanilla, honey, and the rest of the ingredients, stir well and press everything on a baking sheet lined with parchment paper.
2. Keep in the freezer for 30 minutes, cut into 10 squares and serve for breakfast.

Orzo and Veggie Bowls

Preparation:
10'

Cooking:
0'

Servings:
4

NUTRITION
Calories: 411
Fat: 17 gr.
Carbs: 51 gr.
Protein: 14 gr.

INGREDIENTS

- 2 and ½ cups whole-wheat orzo, cooked
- 14 ounces canned cannellini beans, drained and rinsed
- 1 yellow bell pepper, cubed
- 1 green bell pepper, cubed
- A pinch of salt and black pepper
- 3 tomatoes, cubed
- 1 red onion, chopped

- 1 cup mint, chopped
- 2 cups feta cheese, crumbled
- 2 tablespoons olive oil
- ¼ cup lemon juice
- 1 tablespoon lemon zest, grated
- 1 cucumber, cubed
- 1 and ¼ cup kalamata olives, pitted and sliced
- 3 garlic cloves, minced

DIRECTIONS:

1. In a salad bowl, combine the orzo with the beans, bell peppers, and the rest of the ingredients, toss, divide the mix between plates and serve for breakfast.

Lemon Peas Quinoa Mix

Preparation:
10'

Cooking:
20'

Servings:
4

NUTRITION
Calories: 417
Fat: 15 gr.
Carbs: 58 gr.
Protein: 16 gr.

INGREDIENTS

- 1 and ½ cups quinoa, rinsed
- 1-pound asparagus, steamed and chopped
- 3 cups water
- 2 tablespoons parsley, chopped
- 2 tablespoons lemon juice
- 1 teaspoon lemon zest, grated
- ½ pound sugar snap peas, steamed
- ½ pound green beans, trimmed and halved
- A pinch of salt and black pepper
- 3 tablespoons pumpkin seeds
- 1 cup cherry tomatoes, halved
- 2 tablespoons olive oil

DIRECTIONS:

1. Put the water in a pot, bring to a boil over medium heat, add the quinoa, stir, and simmer for 20 minutes.
2. Stir the quinoa, add the parsley, lemon juice, and the rest of the ingredients, toss, divide between plates and serve for breakfast.

Pumpkin Pancakes

INGREDIENTS

- squares puff pastry
- 6 tbsp pumpkin filling
- small eggs, beaten
- ¼ tsp cinnamon

Preparation:
10'

Cooking:
10'

Servings:
8

NUTRITION

Calories: 51

Carbs: 5gr.

Protein: 2.4 gr.

Fat: 2.5 gr.

DIRECTIONS:

1. Preheat the Air fryer to 360 F and roll out a square of puff pastry.
2. Layer it with pumpkin pie filling, leaving about 1/4 -inch space around the edges.
3. Cut it up into equal-sized square pieces and cover the gaps with beaten egg.
4. Arrange the squares into a baking dish and cook for about 12 minutes.
5. Sprinkle some cinnamon and serve

Mediterranean Eggs Cups

Preparation:
10'

Cooking:
20'

Servings:
8

NUTRITION

Calories: 240

Carbs: 13 gr.

Protein: 9 gr.

Fat: 16 gr.

INGREDIENTS

- 1 cup spinach, finely diced
- 1/2 yellow onion, finely diced
- 1/2 cup sliced sun-dried tomatoes
- 4 large basil leaves, finely diced
- Pepper and salt to taste
- 1/3 cup feta cheese crumbles
- 8 large eggs
- 1/4 cup milk (any kind)

DIRECTIONS:

1. You must heat the oven to 375°F.
2. Then, roll the batter sheet into a 12x8-inch square shape
3. Then, cut down the middle the long way
4. From that point forward, you should cut every half across into 4 pieces, framing 8 (4x3-inch) bits of batter. Then, press each into the base and up sides of the ungreased biscuit cup.
5. Trim mixture to hold the batter back from contacting, if fundamental. Put away.
6. Then, you should join the eggs, salt, pepper in the bowl and beat it with a rush until all around blended. Put away.
7. Soften the margarine in a 12-inch skillet over medium hotness until sizzling; add ringer peppers.
8. You should cook it, mixing infrequently, 2-3 minutes or until freshly delicate.
9. From that point onward, add spinach leaves; keep cooking until spinach is shriveled. Then add egg combination and prosciutto.
10. Partition the blend equitably among arranged biscuit cups.
11. Finally, bake it for 14-17 minutes or until the crust is golden brown.

White Breakfast Sandwich with Roasted Tomatoes

Preparation:
10'

Cooking:
15'

Servings:
2

NUTRITION

Calories: 458

Carbs: 51 gr.

Protein: 21 gr.

Fat: 24 gr.

INGREDIENTS

- Salt and pepper to taste
- ¼ cup egg whites
- 1 whole grain seeded ciabatta roll
- 1 teaspoon chopped fresh herbs like rosemary, basil, parsley,
- 1 teaspoon butter
- 1 tablespoon pesto
- 1-2 slices Muenster cheese
- About ½ cup roasted tomatoes
- 10 ounces grape tomatoes
- 1 tablespoon extra-virgin olive oil
- Black pepper and salt to taste

DIRECTIONS:

1. To begin with, you should soften the margarine over medium hotness in the little nonstick skillet.
2. Then, blend the egg whites with pepper and salt at that point.
3. Then, at that point, sprinkle it with the new spices
4. After that, cook it for just about 3-4 minutes or until the eggs are done, then, at that point, flip it cautiously
5. In the meantime, toast crusty bread in the toaster oven
6. From that point forward, you should put the egg on the base portion of the sandwich rolls, then, at that point, top with cheddar
7. Add cooked tomatoes and the top portion of the roll.
8. To make a cooked tomato, preheat the broiler to 400 degrees.
9. Then, at that point, cut the tomatoes in half the long way.
10. Put on the baking sheet and sprinkle with olive oil.
11. Season it with pepper and salt, and afterward cook in the broiler for around 20 minutes. Skins will seem badly creased when done.

Greek Yogurt Pancakes

Preparation:
10'

Cooking:
5'

Servings:
2

NUTRITION
Calories: 165.7
Carbs: 52 gr.
Protein: 14 gr.
Fat: 5 gr.

INGREDIENTS

- 1 cup all-purpose flour
- 1 cup whole-wheat flour
- 1/4 teaspoon salt
- 4 teaspoons baking powder
- 1 Tablespoon sugar
- 1 1/2 cups unsweetened almond milk

- 2 teaspoons vanilla extract
- 2 large eggs
- 1/2 cup plain 2% Greek yogurt
- Fruit, for serving
- Maple syrup, for serving

DIRECTIONS:

1. To start with, you should empty the curds into the bowl and blend them well until rich.
2. You should add egg whites and blend them well until consolidated from that point forward.
3. Then, at that point, take a different bowl, empty the wet combination into the dry blend. Mix to join. The player will be very thick.
4. Then, at that point, just spoon the hitter onto the showered skillet warmed to medium-high.
5. The player should make 4 huge flapjacks.
6. Then, at that point, you should flip the flapjacks once they begin to bubble. Cook until brilliant brown on the two sides.

Mediterranean Feta and Quinoa Egg Muffins

Preparation:
15'

Cooking:
15'

Servings:
12

NUTRITION

Calories: 113kcal

Carbs: 5 gr.

Protein: 6 gr.

Fat: 7 gr.

INGREDIENTS

- 2 cups baby spinach finely chopped
- 1 cup chopped or sliced cherry tomatoes
- 1/2 cup finely chopped onion
- 1 tablespoon chopped fresh oregano
- 1 cup crumbled feta cheese
- 1/2 cup chopped {pitted} kalamata olives
- 2 teaspoons high oleic sunflower oil
- 1 cup cooked quinoa
- 8 eggs
- 1/4 teaspoon salt

DIRECTIONS:

1. Preheat broiler to 350 degrees Fahrenheit, and afterward plan 12 silicone biscuit holders on the baking sheet, or simply oil a 12-cup biscuit tin with oil and put it away.
2. Finely slash the vegetables and afterward heat the skillet to medium.
3. Add the vegetable oil and onions and sauté for 2 minutes from that point forward.
4. Then, at that point, add tomatoes and sauté for one more moment; then, at that point, add spinach and sauté until withered, around 1 moment.
5. Place the beaten egg into a bowl and afterward add heaps of vegetables like feta cheddar, quinoa, veggie combination, and salt. Afterward, mix well until everything is appropriately consolidated.
6. Empty the prepared combination into lubed biscuit tins or silicone cups, isolating the blend similarly. Then, bake it in an oven for 30 minutes or so, or until the eggs set nicely and the muffins turn a light golden brown in color.

Mediterranean Eggs

Preparation:
15'

Cooking:
20'

Servings:
2

NUTRITION
Calories: 304
Carbs: 28 gr.
Protein: 12 gr.
Fat: 16 gr.

INGREDIENTS

- 5 tbsp. of divided olive oil
- 2 diced medium-sized Spanish onions
- 2 diced red bell peppers
- 2 minced cloves garlic
- 1 teaspoon cumin seeds
- 4 diced large ripe tomatoes
- 1 tablespoon of honey

- Salt
- Freshly ground black pepper
- 1/3 cup crumbled feta
- 4 eggs
- 1 teaspoon zaatar spice
- Grilled pita during serving

DIRECTIONS:

1. Most importantly, you should add 3 tablespoons of olive oil into a dish and hotness it over medium hotness. Alongside the oil, sauté the cumin seeds, onions, garlic, and red pepper for a couple of moments.
2. From that point forward, add the diced tomatoes and salt and pepper to taste and cook them for around 10 minutes until they structure a light sauce.
3. With that, a large portion of the arrangement is as of now done. Presently you simply should break the eggs straightforwardly into the sauce and poach them. Notwithstanding, you should remember to cook the egg whites however keep the yolks still runny. This takes around 8 to 10 minutes.
4. While plating, add some feta and olive oil with za'atar spice to further enhance the flavors. Once done, serve with grilled pita.

Chapter 5

Mediterranean Lunch Recipes

Lentil, Shrimp and Bean Salad

Preparation:
10'

Cooking:
5'

Servings:
4

NUTRITION

Calories: 347

Carbs: 38 gr.

Protein: 19.5 gr.

Fat: 8.9 gr.

INGREDIENTS

- 0.5 bell pepper, chopped
- 5-7 mint leaves, chopped
- 2 tsp capers
- 2 tsp garlic, minced
- 1 can brown lentils ~15 oz
- 7 oz cooked shrimp

- 2 tbsp white wine vinegar
- 1 can white beans ~15 oz
- salt and black pepper to taste
- 2 tbsp extra virgin olive oil
- 0.5 tsp ground cumin
- 0.5 tsp paprika

DIRECTIONS:

1. Mix the shrimp, pepper, capers, white beans, lentils, mint, and minced garlic together.
2. Season with the spices and add the white wine vinegar and olive oil as a dressing.
3. Stir so everything is well designed.
4. This is a great meal with a slice of your favorite whole wheat pita bread.

Creamy Chicken Breast

INGREDIENTS

Preparation:
10'

Cooking:
20'

Servings:
4

- A pinch of black pepper
- 1 tablespoon olive oil
- 4 garlic cloves, minced
- ½ cup low-Fat parmesan, grated
- 2 pounds chicken breasts, skinless, boneless, and cubed
- 2 and ½ cups low-sodium chicken stock
- 2 cups coconut cream
- 1 tablespoon basil, chopped

NUTRITION

Calories 221

Carbs: 14 gr.

Protein: 7gr.

Fat: 6 gr.

DIRECTIONS:

1. Heat-up a dish with the oil over medium-high hotness, add chicken blocks, and earthy colored them for 3 minutes on each side. Add garlic, dark pepper, stock, and cream, throw, cover the dish, and cook everything for 10 minutes more. Add cheddar and basil, throw, split among plates, and serve for lunch.

Quinoa Chicken Salad

Preparation:
15'

Cooking:
20'

Servings:
8

NUTRITION
Calories: 99
Carbs: 7 gr.
Protein: 3.4 gr.
Fat: 7 gr.

INGREDIENTS

- 2 cups of water
- 2 cubes of chicken bouillon
- 1 smashed garlic clove
- 1 cup of uncooked quinoa
- 2 large-sized chicken breasts cut up into bite-sized portions and cooked
- 1 large-sized diced red onion
- 1 large-sized green bell pepper
- ½ cup of crumbled feta cheese
- ½ cup of Kalamata olives
- ½ teaspoon of salt
- ¼ cup of chopped up parsley
- ¼ cup of chopped up fresh chives
- 1 tablespoon of balsamic vinegar
- ¼ cup of olive oil

DIRECTIONS:

1. Take a pan and bring your water, garlic, and bouillon 3D shapes to a bubble. Mix in quinoa and lessen the hotness to medium-low.
2. Stew for around 15-20 minutes until the quinoa has retained all the water and is delicate. Dispose of your garlic cloves and scratch the quinoa into a huge measured bowl.
3. Delicately mix in the cooked chicken bosom, chime pepper, onion, feta cheddar, chives, salt, and parsley into your quinoa.
4. Sprinkle some lemon juice, olive oil, and balsamic vinegar. Mix everything until blended well.

Purple Potato Soup

Preparation:
10'

Cooking:
1 h 15'

Servings:
6

NUTRITION
Calories: 70
Carbs: 15 gr.
Protein: 2 gr.
Fat: 0 gr.

INGREDIENTS

- 4 garlic cloves, minced
- 1 yellow onion, chopped
- 6 purple potatoes, chopped
- 3 tablespoons olive oil
- 1 cauliflower head, florets separated
- Black pepper to the taste
- 1 tablespoon thyme, chopped
- 1 leek, chopped
- 2 shallots, chopped
- 4 cups chicken stock, low-sodium

DIRECTIONS:

1. In a baking dish, blend potatoes in with the onion, cauliflower, garlic, pepper, thyme, and a big part of the oil, throw to cover, present in the stove, and prepare for 45 minutes at 400 degrees F.
2. Heat a pot with the remainder of the oil over medium-high hotness, add leeks and shallots, mix, and cook for 10 minutes.
3. Add broiled veggies and stock, mix, heat to the point of boiling, cook for 20 minutes, move soup to your food processor, mix well, partition into bowls, and serve.

Light Balsamic Salad

Preparation:
10'

Cooking:
0'

Servings:
3

NUTRITION
Calories: 35
Carbs: 5g
Protein: 0g
Fat: 2g

INGREDIENTS

- 1 orange, cut into segments
- 2 green onions, chopped
- 1 romaine lettuce head, torn
- 1 avocado, pitted, peeled, and cubed
- ¼ cup almonds, sliced

for the salad dressing:
- 1 teaspoon mustard
- ¼ cup olive oil
- 2 tablespoons balsamic vinegar
- Juice of½ orange
- Salt and black pepper

DIRECTIONS:

1. Mix oranges with avocado, lettuce, almonds, and green onions in a salad bowl. In another bowl, mix olive oil with vinegar, mustard, orange juice, salt, and pepper, whisk well, add this to your salad, toss and serve.

Leeks Soup

Preparation:
10'

Cooking:
1 h 15'

Servings:
6

NUTRITION

Calories: 125

Carbs: 29 gr.

Protein: 4 gr.

Fat: 1 gr.

INGREDIENTS

- 1 cup cauliflower florets
- 2 gold potatoes, chopped Black pepper to the taste
- 4 garlic cloves, minced
- 5 leeks, chopped
- Handful parsley, chopped

- 1 yellow onion, chopped
- 3 tablespoons olive oil
- 4 cups low-sodium chicken stock

DIRECTIONS:

1. Heat up a pot with the oil over medium-high hotness, add onion and garlic, mix, and cook for 5 minutes.
2. Add potatoes, cauliflower, dark pepper, leeks, and stock, mix, bring to a stew, cook over medium hotness for 30 minutes, mix utilizing a submersion blender, add parsley, mix, scoop into bowls and serve.

Cauliflower Lunch Salad

Preparation:
2 h

Cooking:
10'

Servings:
4

NUTRITION
Calories: 102
Carbs: 3 gr.
Protein: 0 gr.
Fat: 10 gr.

INGREDIENTS

- 2 tablespoons olive oil
- Black pepper to the taste
- 1/3 cup low-sodium veggie stock
- 6 cups cauliflower florets, grated
- Juice of ½ lemon

- ¼ cup red onion chopped
- 1 red bell pepper, chopped
- ½ cup kalamata olives halved
- 1 teaspoon mint, chopped
- 1 tablespoon cilantro, chopped

DIRECTIONS:

1. Heat up a pan with the oil over medium-high heat, add cauliflower, pepper, and stock, stir, cook within 10 minutes, move to a bowl, and keep in the ice chest for 2 hours. Blend cauliflower in with olives, onion, ringer pepper, dark pepper, mint, cilantro, and lemon juice, throw to cover and serve.

Easy Lunch Salmon Steaks

Preparation:
10'

Cooking:
20'

Servings:
4

INGREDIENTS

- 1 big salmon fillet, cut into 4 steaks,
- 3 garlic cloves, minced
- 1 yellow onion, chopped Black pepper to the taste,
- 2 tablespoons olive oil
- ¼ cup parsley, chopped
- Juice of 1 lemon
- 1 tablespoon thyme, chopped
- 4 cups of water

NUTRITION
Calories: 110
Carbs: 3 gr.
Protein: 15 gr.
Fat: 4 gr.

DIRECTIONS:

1. Heat a pan with the oil on medium-high heat, cook onion and garlic within 3 minutes.
2. Add black pepper, parsley, thyme, water, and lemon juice, stir, bring to a gentle boil, add salmon steaks, cook them for 15 minutes, drain, divide between plates, and serve with a side salad for lunch.

Sweet Potatoes and Zucchini Soup

Preparation:
10'

Cooking:
20'

Servings:
8

NUTRITION

Calories: 270

Carbs: 50 gr.

Protein: 11 gr.

Fat: 4 gr.

INGREDIENTS

- 4 cups veggie stock
- 2 tablespoons olive oil
- 2 sweet potatoes, peeled and cubed
- 8 zucchinis, chopped
- 2 yellow onions, chopped
- 1 cup of coconut milk
- A pinch of black pepper
- 1 tablespoon coconut aminos
- 4 tablespoons dill, chopped
- ½ teaspoon basil, chopped

DIRECTIONS:

1. Heat up a pot with the oil over medium heat, add onion, stir, and cook for 5 minutes. Add zucchinis, stock, basil, potato, and pepper, stir, and cook for 15 minutes more. Add milk, aminos, and dill, pulse using an immersion blender, ladle into bowls and serve for lunch.

Rice with Chicken

Preparation:
10'

Cooking:
30'

Servings:
4

NUTRITION
Calories: 70
Carbs: 13 gr.
Protein: 2 gr.
Fat: 2 gr.

INGREDIENTS

- 1/3 cup rice wine vinegar
- 1 chicken breast, skinless, boneless, and cubed
- ½ cup coconut aminos
- 2 tablespoons olive oil
- A pinch of black pepper
- ½ cup red bell pepper, chopped
- ½ cup carrots, grated
- 2 garlic cloves, minced
- ½ teaspoon ginger, grated
- 1 cup white rice
- 2 cups of water

DIRECTIONS:

1. Heat up a skillet with the oil over medium-high hotness, add the chicken, mix, and brown for 4 minutes on each side. Add aminos, vinegar, ringer pepper, dark pepper, garlic, ginger, carrots, rice, and stock, cover the skillet and cook over medium hotness for 20 minutes. Partition everything into bowls and serve for lunch.

Spinach and egg scramble with raspberries

Preparation:
10'

Cooking:
10'

Servings:
1

NUTRITION
Calories: 296
Carbs: 21 gr.
Protein: 18 gr.
Fat: 16 gr.

INGREDIENTS

- 1 teaspoon of canola oil
- 1 and 1/2 cups of baby spinach (which is one and a half ounces)
- 2 eggs, large and lightly beaten
- salt, a pinch.
- Ground pepper, a pinch
- 1 slice of whole-grain toasted bread
- 1/2 cup of fresh and fine raspberries

DIRECTIONS:

1. Heat the oil in a nonstick and little skillet at a temperature of medium-high.
2. Add spinach to the plate.
3. Neatly wipe the dish and add eggs into the medium warmed skillet.
4. Mix and cook two times to guarantee even-cooking for around two minutes.
5. Mix the spinach in and add salt and pepper into it.
6. Embellish it with raspberries and toast prior to eating.

Mediterranean lettuce wraps

Preparation:
10'

Cooking:
10'

Servings:
4

NUTRITION
Calories: 498
Carbs: 44 gr.
Protein: 16 gr.
Fat: 28 gr.

INGREDIENTS

- 1/4 cup of tahini
- 1/4 cup of olive oil, extra-virgin
- 1 teaspoon of lemon zest
- 1/4 cup of lemon juice
- 1 and 1/2 tsp. of pure maple syrup
- 3/4 tsp. of kosher salt
- 1/2 tsp. of paprika
- 2 cans (15 ounces) of rinsed chickpeas, no-salt-added

- 1/2 cup of sliced and roasted red pepper - drained and jarred
- 1/2 cup of thinly sliced shallots
- 2 tsp. of fresh parsley, chopped
- 12 leaves of Bibb lettuce, large
- 1/4 cup of almonds, roasted and chopped

DIRECTIONS:

1. Whisk lemon zing, tahini, oil, maple syrup, lemon juice, paprika, and all in a bowl.
2. After which, add peppers, chickpeas, and shallots.
3. Presently, throw for covering.
4. After this, split this blend between the lettuce leaves (say around 33% cup for each part).
5. Top with parsley and almonds.
6. Prior to serving, wrap lettuce leaves around this filling for appropriate embellishing.

Pressed Tuna Sandwich

Preparation:
40'

Cooking:
2 h 40'

Servings:
8

NUTRITION
Calories: 266
Carbs: 23 g
Protein: 13 g
Fat: 12 g

INGREDIENTS

- ½ cup of red onion, thinly sliced
- 5 tsp. of divided red-wine vinegar, divided
- 2 tsp. of boiling water
- 12 inches of the crusty country loaf, whole-wheat should be taken about one pound
- 2 tsp. of olive oil, extra-virgin
- 1 tsp. of Dijon mustard
- ½ tsp. of pepper, ground
- 1/4 tsp. of salt
- 2 cans or five ounces of chunk and drained light tuna, oil-packed
- 1 cup of baby arugula, packed
- 1 cup of English cucumber, thinly sliced
- 1 cup of radishes, thinly sliced
- 1 cup of quartered cherry tomatoes
- 1/2 cup of olives pitted and unevenly chopped
- 4 thinly sliced boiled eggs, hard and large
- 1/4 cup of fresh basil, packed

DIRECTIONS:

1. Consolidate two tsp of vinegar, water, and onions into one little bowl.
2. Marinate and mix for ten minutes.
3. Slice level portions down the middle.
4. Take out internal bread from the parts by leaving around a large portion of an inch.
5. Whisk three tsp of vinegar, oil, pepper, salt, and mustard in one bowl.
6. Channel the onion and add arugula, fish, radishes, cucumber, olives, and tomatoes.
7. Stuff the blend into the base portion of one portion.
8. Top with basil, eggs, and the portion's top.
9. Refrigerate for two hours.

Mediterranean Chicken Panini

Preparation:
25'

Cooking:
35'

Servings:
4

NUTRITION
Calories: 216
Carbs: 31 gr.
Protein: 19 gr.
Fat: 3 gr.

INGREDIENTS

- Nonstick Olive oil spray for cooking
- 2 skinless and boneless breast halves of a chicken, small
- 1/3 cup of dried tomatoes
- 3 tsp. of boiling water
- 1/3 cup of red sweet peppers, bottled roasted, and drained
- 4 tsp. of vinegar, balsamic
- 1 tsp. of oregano snipped fresh or half tsp. of crushed oregano, dried
- 1 clove garlic, large and minced
- 1/8 tsp. of black pepper, ground
- 4 whole wheat, miniature squares, and bagel bread or split ciabatta rolls, multigrain
- 1 zucchini, small

DIRECTIONS:

1. Coat an unheated large nonstick skillet with cooking spray
2. Preheat and add chicken.
3. Cook chicken for about twelve minutes.
4. Cool chicken and split each piece in on a level plane half and cut into 2-inch cuts, transversely.
5. Consolidate and cover bubbling water and dried tomatoes for 5 minutes.
6. Move un-depleted, blend in little processor, and add red sweet peppers, oregano, balsamic vinegar, ground dark pepper, clove garlic, and cover.
7. Spread dried spread on bagel bread squares' cut sides.
8. Put chicken on the lower part of the bread.
9. Cut slender strips from zucchini and put on chicken's top.
10. Place weighty skillet sandwiches and cook for 2 minutes. Turn the sandwich and cook for an additional two minutes.
11. Turn the sandwich and cook for another two minutes.

Mediterranean Veggie Wrap with Cilantro

Preparation:
20'

Cooking:
20'

Servings:
2

NUTRITION

Calories: 269

Carbs: 35 gr.

Protein: 16 gr.

Fat: 12 gr.

INGREDIENTS

- Spinach or tomato-basil wrap (1 (9-inch))
- Chopped fresh baby spinach (3/4 cup)
- One third less Fat cream cheese (1 tablespoon)
- Crumbled feta cheese (1/3 cup)
- Avocado, sliced (1/2 small)
- Chopped tomato (1/4 cup)
- Cilantro, sliced (1/2 small)
- Chopped fresh basil (1 to 1 1/2 tablespoons)
- Wine vinaigrette (1 tablespoon)
- Sliced black olives (2 tablespoons)

DIRECTIONS:

1. Spread the cream cheese on only one side of the wrap. Be generous with the cheese, as this will give a creamy texture to the wrap.
2. Top the cheese with chopped spinach as well as the other ingredients.
3. Make a proper hummus with cilantro. This is the major flavor that is the highlight of the wrap.
4. Add the hummus into the wrap, and then it is almost ready.
5. The major step is to roll the wrap properly. Make sure it is tight, but the ingredients don't fall out.
6. Blush the wrap with wine vinaigrette as it will give a proper color to the wrap.
7. Cut the wrap into two and serve them.

Shrimp, Avocado and Feta Wrap

Preparation:
5'

Cooking:
5'

Servings:
2

NUTRITION

Calories: 371

Carbs: 34 gr.

Protein: 29 gr.

Fat: 14 gr.

INGREDIENTS

- Chopped cooked shrimp (3 ounces)
- Lime juice (1 tablespoon)
- Crumbled feta cheese (2 tablespoons)
- Diced avocado (¼ cup)
- Whole-wheat tortilla (1 piece)
- Diced tomato (¼ cup)
- Sliced scallion (1 Piece)

DIRECTIONS:

1. Spray vegetable oil on a skillet and then heat it. Add the shrimp to get a nice pink color to them.
2. Add the feta cheese on one side of the wrap and be generous with the cheese.
3. Top the cheese with various other ingredients. Add the shrimp on the top so they will be in the middle of the wrap when you roll it.
4. Add lime juice to give it the tangy zing to the wrap.
5. Then roll the wrap tightly, but make sure that the ingredients don't fall off.
6. Then cut the wrap into two halves and serve it.

Tomato, Cucumber and White Bean Salad

Preparation:
25'

Cooking:
25'

Servings:
4

INGREDIENTS

- ¼ teaspoon of salt
- ¼ teaspoon of ground pepper
- 10 cups of mixed salad greens
- 1 can (or 15 ounces) of low-sodium cannellini beans, rinsed
- 1 cup of halved cherry or grape tomatoes
- 1 cup of half cucumber halved lengthwise and sliced
- 3 tablespoons of red wine vinegar
- 1 tablespoon of finely chopped shallot
- 2 teaspoons of Dijon mustard
- A ½ cup of fresh packed basil leaves
- A ¼ cup of extra-virgin olive oil

NUTRITION
Calories: 246
Carbs: 22 gr.
Protein: 8 gr.
Fat: 15 gr.

DIRECTIONS:

1. The making of the smooth paste is the most important part of the recipe.
2. Add the oil, basil, shallot, vinegar, mustard, salt, honey, and pepper in a food processor and churn them till it becomes a smooth paste.
3. Transfer the pate into a large bowl. This is the base of the basic recipe, and you are almost halfway done with the food.
4. Add the green vegetables, tomatoes, beans, and cucumber onto the paste. This is all the ingredients in the recipe.
5. Toss the bowl and its ingredients to coat the ingredients with the smooth paste.

Italian Herbed Chicken and Mozzarella

Preparation:
20'

Cooking:
3 h 35'

Servings:
4

NUTRITION

Calories: 367.9

Carbs: 24.5 gr.

Protein: 33.0 gr.

Fat: 16.1 gr.

INGREDIENTS

- 1 cup of part-skim shredded mozzarella cheese (about 4 ounces)
- A ¼ cup of snipped fresh basil
- 2 tablespoons of grated Parmesan cheese
- 8 slices of whole-grain Italian bread
- 8 pieces of skinless, boneless chicken thighs
- 2 pieces of medium green sweet peppers, thinly sliced
- ½ teaspoon of dried rosemary, it should be crushed
- 1 cup of bottled spaghetti sauce

DIRECTIONS:

1. Pat the chicken with paper towels till it is dry.
2. Marinate the chicken with seasoning and other ingredients.
3. Leave the marinated chicken at room temperature for about fifteen to twenty minutes.
4. Add olive oil and then roast the rosemary, onion, garlic, and thyme in them. Also, season them and roast them for about twenty minutes.
5. Mix tomatoes, vinegar, and sugar in a pot, simmer for ten minutes, and bring to boil.
6. Add olive oil in a frying pan and then fry them till they are brown on both sides. There is no need to cook it entirely through.
7. Add the chicken and the vegetables with all the ingredients in a baking dish and add tomato sauce with mozzarella. Then, bake for about ten minutes and grill for about three minutes. You are then ready to go.

Mediterranean Egg and Tomato Skillet with Pita

Preparation:
30'

Cooking:
40'

Servings:
2

NUTRITION
Calories: 303
Carbs: 33 gr.
Protein: 15 gr.
Fat: 13 gr.

INGREDIENTS

- 1 teaspoon of ground cumin
- 4 pieces of eggs
- ¼ teaspoon of salt
- Snipped fresh parsley
- A ½ cup of plain low-Fat Greek yogurt
- 2 tablespoons of olive oil
- 2 whole-wheat pita bread rounds, warmed
- 2 tablespoons of tomato paste without salt
- 2 cups of chopped red sweet peppers
- A ½ cup of chopped onion
- 2 teaspoons of crushed red pepper
- 1 teaspoon smoked paprika
- 3 cups chopped tomatoes

DIRECTIONS:

1. Heat a skillet with oil and then add the onions, peppers, parsley. Cook them on medium heat for five to seven minutes till the onions get soft.
2. Add the tomatoes, salt, and cumin and stir it properly. Bring it to a boil and then reduce it. After that, simmer it for about ten minutes.
3. Make four indentations in the tomato sauce, and then slip the eggs into these indentations. Cover the vessel and let it cook for four to six minutes.
4. Add yogurt as a topping and sprinkle it with parsley on top.
5. You should serve it with pita bread as this is a great combination.

Chapter 6

Mediterranean Dinner Recipes

Walnut-Rosemary Crusted Salmon

Preparation:
10'

Cooking:
20'

Servings:
4

NUTRITION
Calories: 222
Carbs: 4 gr.
Protein: 24 gr.
Fat: 12 gr.

INGREDIENTS

- 2 teaspoons of Dijon mustard
- 1 minced clove garlic
- ¼ teaspoon of lemon zest
- ½ teaspoon of honey
- ½ teaspoon of kosher salt
- 1 teaspoon of chopped fresh rosemary
- 3 tablespoons of panko breadcrumbs
- ¼ teaspoon of crushed red pepper
- 3 tablespoons of finely chopped walnuts
- 1 pound of frozen or fresh skinless salmon fillet
- 1 teaspoon of extra-virgin olive oil
- Olive oil

DIRECTIONS:

1. Preheat the oven to 420°F and use parchment paper to line a rimmed baking sheet.
2. Combine mustard, lemon zest, garlic, lemon juice, honey, rosemary, crushed red pepper, and salt in a bowl.
3. Combine walnuts and panko, with oil, in another bowl.
4. Place the salmon on that baking sheet. Spread that mustard mix on the fish, along with the panko mix. Make sure the fish is adequately coated with the mixtures. Spray olive oil lightly on the salmon.
5. Bake for about 8-12 minutes (till the salmon can be separated using a fork).

Caprese Stuffed Portobello Mushrooms

Preparation:
25'

Cooking:
40'

Servings:
2

NUTRITION

Calories: 186
Carbs: 6 gr.
Protein: 6 gr.
Fat: 16 gr.

INGREDIENTS

- 3 tablespoons of divided extra-virgin olive oil
- 1 medium minced clove garlic
- ½ teaspoon of salt
- ½ teaspoon of ground pepper
- About 14 ounces of Portobello mushrooms, with gills and stems, removed

- 1 cup of halved cherry tomatoes
- A ½ cup of fresh and drained mozzarella pearls patted dry
- A ½ cup of thinly sliced fresh basil
- 2 teaspoons of balsamic vinegar

DIRECTIONS:

1. Preheat the oven to 400°F. Combine a ¼ teaspoon of salt, two tablespoons of oil, and a ¼ teaspoon of pepper in a bowl. Utilize a brush to cover the mushrooms with this combination.
2. Place the mushrooms on a baking sheet and bake them for about ten minutes (till the mushrooms get soft).
3. Stir basil, tomatoes, and mozzarella in a pan. Mix 1 tablespoon of oil, a ¼ teaspoon of salt, and a ¼ teaspoon of pepper in a bowl.
4. Remove the components of the pan after the mushrooms soften. Fill the mushrooms with the tomato mix.
5. Bake till the tomatoes wilt and the cheese melts, for about 15 minutes. Drizzle the mushrooms with half teaspoons of vinegar before serving.

Greek Salad Nachos

Preparation:
15'

Cooking:
15'

Servings:
6

NUTRITION
Calories: 159
Carbs: 13 gr.
Protein: 4 gr.
Fat: 10 gr.

INGREDIENTS

- 1/3 cup of hummus
- 2 tablespoons of extra-virgin olive oil
- 1 tablespoon of lemon juice
- ¼ teaspoon of ground pepper
- 3 cups of whole-grain pita chips
- 1 cup of chopped lettuce
- A ½ cup of quartered grape tomatoes
- A ¼ cup of crumbled feta cheese
- 2 tablespoons of chopped olives
- 2 tablespoons of minced red onion
- 1 tablespoon of minced fresh oregano

DIRECTIONS:

1. Whisk pepper, lemon juice, oil, and hummus in a bowl.
2. Spread the pita chips on a plate in one layer.
3. Cover the chips with about ¾ of that hummus mix and top it with tomatoes, red onion, olives, feta, and lettuce. Cover it with the rest of the hummus. Sprinkle oregano on top before serving it.

Greek Chicken with Lemon Vinaigrette and Roasted Spring Vegetables

Preparation:

30'

Cooking:

50'

Servings:

4

INGREDIENTS

For the lemon vinaigrette
- 1 lemon
- 1 tablespoon olive oil
- 1 tablespoon crumbled feta cheese
- ½ teaspoon honey

For the Greek Chicken and roasted veggies
- 8 ounce of boneless, skinless chicken breast, cut lengthwise in half
- A ¼ cup of light mayonnaise

- 6 cloves of minced garlic
- A ½ cup of panko breadcrumbs
- 3 tablespoons of grated Parmesan cheese
- ½ teaspoon of kosher salt
- ½ teaspoon of black pepper
- 1-inch pieces of asparagus, 2 cups
- 1½ cups of sliced cremini mushrooms
- 1½ cups of halved cherry tomatoes
- 1 tablespoon of olive oil

NUTRITION
Calories: 306
Carbs: 12 gr.
Protein: 29 gr.
Fat: 15 gr.

DIRECTIONS:

1. Put half teaspoons of zest, one tablespoon of lemon juice, olive oil, cheese, and honey in a bowl to make the vinaigrette.
2. For the vegetables and chicken, preheat the oven to 470°F. Use a meat mallet for flattening the chicken between two pieces of plastic wrap.
3. Place the chicken in a bowl and add two garlic cloves and mayonnaise. Mix cheese, breadcrumbs, a ¼ teaspoon of pepper, and a ¼ teaspoon of salt together. Dip the chicken in this crumb mix. Spray olive oil over the chicken.
4. Roast in the oven till the chicken is done and vegetables are tender. Sprinkle dill over it and serve.

Chicken in Tomato-Balsamic Pan Sauce

Preparation:
35'

Cooking:
35'

Servings:
4

INGREDIENTS

- 2 8-ounce skinless, boneless chicken breasts
- ½ teaspoon of salt
- ½ teaspoon of ground pepper
- 2 tablespoons of corn
- A ¼ cup of white whole-wheat flour
- 3 tablespoons of extra-virgin olive oil
- A ½ cup of halved cherry tomatoes
- 2 tablespoons of sliced shallot
- A ¼ cup of balsamic vinegar
- 1 cup of low-sodium chicken broth
- 1 tablespoon of minced garlic
- 1 tablespoon of toasted and crushed fennel seeds
- 1 tablespoon of butter

NUTRITION
Calories: 294
Carbs: 9 gr.
Protein: 25 gr.
Fat: 17 gr.

DIRECTIONS:

1. Slice the chicken breasts into 4 pieces and beat them with a mallet till it reaches a thickness of a ¼ inch. Use ¼ teaspoons of pepper and salt to coat the chicken.
2. Heat two tablespoons of oil in a skillet and keep the heat to a medium. Cook the chicken breasts for two minutes on each side. Transfer it to a serving plate and cover it with foil to keep it warm.
3. Add one tablespoon oil, shallot, and tomatoes in a pan and cook till it softens. Add vinegar and boil the mix till the vinegar gets reduced by half. Put fennel seeds, garlic, corn, salt, and pepper and cook for about four minutes. Remove it from the heat and stir it with butter.
4. Pour this sauce over the chicken and serve.

Chicken Souvlaki Kebabs
with Mediterranean Couscous

Preparation:
45'

Cooking:
2 h 20'

Servings:
4

INGREDIENTS

For the Kebabs-
- 1 pound of boneless, skinless chicken breast halves in ½-inch strips
- 1 cup of sliced fennel
- 1/3 Cup of dry white wine
- A ¼ cup of lemon juice
- 3 tablespoons of canola oil
- 4 cloves of garlic, minced
- 2 teaspoons dried and crushed oregano
- ½ teaspoon salt
- ¼ teaspoon black pepper

Couscous-
- 1 teaspoon of olive oil
- A ½ cup of Israeli couscous
- 1 cup of water
- A ½ cup of snipped dried tomatoes
- A ¾ cup of chopped red sweet pepper
- ½ cup each of chopped cucumber and red onion
- 1/3 Cup of plain Fat-free Greek yogurt
- A ¼ cup of fresh basil leaves, thinly sliced
- A ¼ cup of snipped fresh parsley
- 1 tablespoon of lemon juice
- ¼ teaspoon of salt
- ¼ teaspoon of black pepper

NUTRITION
Calories: 322
Carbs: 28 gr.
Protein: 32 gr.
Fat: 9 gr.

DIRECTIONS:

1. Place chicken with sliced fennel in a sealable plastic bag and set aside. Combine the lemon juice, white wine, oil, oregano, garlic, pepper, and salt in a bowl for the marinade. Take a ¼ cup of this marinade and set it aside.
2. Pour the rest of the marinade over the chicken and refrigerate for 1 ½ hour.
3. Take wooden skewers and thread chicken onto it in accordion style.
4. Grill the chicken skewers for six to eight minutes.
5. Put all the ingredients of couscous in a pan and cook it in olive oil. Serve it alongside the chicken.

Caprese Chicken Hasselback style

Preparation:
25'

Cooking:
50'

Servings:
4

NUTRITION

Calories: 355
Carbs: 10 gr.
Protein: 38 gr.
Fat: 19 gr.

INGREDIENTS

- 2 skinless, boneless chicken breasts - 8 ounces each
- ½ teaspoon of salt
- ½ teaspoon of ground pepper
- 1 medium tomato, sliced
- 3 ounces of fresh mozzarella, halved and sliced
- A ¼ cup of prepared pesto
- 8 cups of broccoli florets
- 2 tablespoons of olive oil

DIRECTIONS:

1. Preheat the oven to 375°F and coat a rimmed baking sheet with cooking spray.
2. Make crosswire cuts at half inches in the chicken breasts. Sprinkle pepper and salt on them. Fill the cuts with mozzarella slices and tomato alternatively. Brush both the chicken breasts with pesto and put them on the baking sheet.
3. Mix broccoli, oil, salt, and pepper in a bowl. Put in the tomatoes if there are any left. Put this mixture on one side of the baking sheet.
4. Bake till the broccoli is tender and the chicken is not pink in the center. Cut each of the breasts in half and serve.

Simple Grilled Salmon with Veggies

Preparation:
25'

Cooking:
25'

Servings:
4

NUTRITION
Calories: 186
Carbs: 6 gr.
Protein: 6 gr.
Fat: 16 gr.

INGREDIENTS

- 1 medium zucchini, lengthwise halved
- 2 orange, red, or yellow bell peppers, halved, trimmed, and seeded
- 1 medium red onion, cut into wedges of 1-inch

- 1 tablespoon of olive oil
- ½ teaspoon salt and ground pepper
- 1¼ pounds salmon fillet, cut into 4 pieces
- ¼ cup thinly sliced fresh basil
- 1 lemon, cut into 4 wedges

DIRECTIONS:

1. Preheat the grill to medium-high. Brush peppers, zucchini, and onion with oil. Sprinkle a ¼ teaspoon of salt over it. Sprinkle salmon with salt and pepper.
2. Place the veggies and the salmon on the grill. Cook the veggies for six to eight minutes on each side, till the grill marks appear. Cook the salmon till it flakes when you test it with a fork.
3. When cooled down, chop the veggies roughly and mix them together in a bowl. You can remove the salmon skin to serve with the veggies. Each serving can be garnished with a tablespoon of basil and a lemon wedge.

Greek Turkey Burgers with Spinach, Feta & Tzatziki

Preparation:
30'

Cooking:
30'

Servings:
4

NUTRITION
Calories: 376
Carbs: 28 gr.
Protein: 30 gr.
Fat: 17 gr.

INGREDIENTS

- 1 cup of chopped spinach, frozen and thawed
- 1 pound of lean 93% turkey, ground
- 1/2 cup of feta cheese, crumbled
- 1/2 tsp. of garlic powder
- 1/2 tsp. of oregano, dried
- 1/4 tsp. of salt
- ¼ tsp. of pepper, ground
- 4 hamburger buns, small and whole-wheat
- 4 tsp. of tzatziki
- 12 slices of cucumber
- 8 red onion, thick rings

DIRECTIONS:

1. Preheat the grill to med high.
2. Squeeze moisture from spinach and combine it with turkey, garlic powder, feta, pepper, and salt in a bowl to mix well.
3. Form 4 four inches of patties and oil the grill rack.
4. When cooked, grill patties for four to six minutes for each side until the thermometer reads 165°F.
5. Assemble burgers on buns and top each with 1 tsp of tzatziki, two onion rings, and three cucumbers.
6. Wrap them and refrigerate them for eight hours.

Mediterranean Chicken Quinoa Bowl

Preparation:
30'

Cooking:
30'

Servings:
4

INGREDIENTS

- 1 pound of skinless and boneless trimmed chicken breasts
- 1/4 tsp. of salt
- 1/4 tsp. of pepper, ground
- 1 seven-ounce jar of red pepper, rinsed and roasted
- 1/4 cup of almonds, slivered
- 4 tsp. of olive oil, extra-virgin and divided

- 1/2 tsp. of cumin, ground
- 1/4 tsp. of red pepper, crushed
- 2 cups of quinoa, cooked
- 1/4 cup of Kalamata olives, pitted and chopped
- 1/4 cup of red onion, finely chopped
- 1 cup of cucumber, diced
- 1/4 cup of feta cheese, crumbled
- 2 tsp. of fresh parsley, finely chopped

NUTRITION
Calories: 519
Carbs: 31 gr.
Protein: 34 gr.
Fat: 27 gr.

DIRECTIONS:

1. Place a rack in the oven and preheat to lime rimmed baking sheet along with foil
2. Sprinkle the chicken with pepper and salt to place on the baking sheet. Broil until the thermometer reads 165°F. Then transfer chicken to a cutting board.
3. Place almonds, oil, pepper, cumin, red pepper, paprika together and puree it.
4. Combine olives, quinoa, red onion, and the remaining two tablespoons of oil in a bowl.
5. Before serving, sprinkle the dish with parsley and feta.

Cajun Jambalaya Soup

Preparation:
25'

Cooking:
6 h

Servings:
6

INGREDIENTS

- ¼ cup Frank's red-hot sauce
- 3 tbsp Cajun seasoning
- 2 cups okra
- ½ head of cauliflower
- 1 pkg spicy Andouille sausages
- 4 oz chicken, diced
- 1 lb. large shrimps, raw and deveined

- 2 bay leaves
- 2 cloves garlic, diced
- 1 large can of organic diced tomatoes
- 1 large onion, chopped
- 4 peppers
- 5 cups chicken stock

NUTRITION
Calories: 155
Carbs: 13.9 gr.
Protein: 17.4 gr.
Fat: 3.8 gr.

DIRECTIONS:

1. In a slow cooker, place the bay leaves, red hot sauce, Cajun seasoning, chicken, garlic, onions, and peppers.
2. Set slow cooker on low and cook for 5 ½ hours.
3. Then add sausages cook for 10 minutes.
4. Meanwhile, pulse cauliflower in a food processor to make cauliflower rice.
5. Add cauliflower rice into the slow cooker. Cook for 20 minutes.
6. Serve and enjoy.

Chapter 7

Mediterranean Vegetable Recipes

Basil and Tomato Soup

Preparation:
15'

Cooking:
25'

Servings:
2

INGREDIENTS

- Salt and pepper to taste
- 2 bay leaves
- 1 ½ cups almond milk, unsweetened
- ½ tsp raw apple cider vinegar
- 1/3 cup basil leaves
- ¼ cup tomato paste
- 3 cups tomatoes, chopped
- 1 medium celery stalk, chopped
- 1 medium carrot, chopped
- 1 medium garlic clove, minced
- ½ cup white onion
- 2 tbsp vegetable broth

NUTRITION
Calories: 213
Carbs: 42.0 gr.
Protein: 6.9 gr.
Fat: 3.9 gr.

DIRECTIONS:

1. Heat the vegetable broth in a large saucepan over medium heat.
2. Add the onions and cook for 3 minutes. Add the garlic and cook for one more moment.
3. Add the celery and carrots and cook for 1 moment.
4. Blend in the tomatoes and heat to the point of boiling.
5. Simmer for 15 minutes.
6. Add the almond milk, basil, and bay leaves. Season with salt and pepper to taste.

Butternut Squash Hummus

INGREDIENTS

- 2 pounds butternut squash, seeded and peeled
- 1 tablespoon olive oil
- ¼ cup tahini
- 2 tablespoons lemon juice
- 2 cloves of garlic, minced
- Salt and pepper to taste

Preparation:
10'

Cooking:
15'

Servings:
8

NUTRITION

Calories: 115
Carbs: 15.8 gr.
Protein: 2.5 gr.
Fat: 5.8 gr.
Fiber: 6.7 gr.

DIRECTIONS:

1. Heat the oven to 3000F.
2. Coat the butternut squash with olive oil.
3. Place in a baking dish and bake for 15 minutes in the oven.
4. Once the squash is cooked, place it in a food processor together with the rest of the ingredients.
5. Pulse until smooth.
6. Place in individual containers.
7. Put a label and store it in the fridge.
8. Allow warming at room temperature before heating in the microwave oven.
9. Serve with carrots or celery sticks.

Collard Green Wrap Greek Style

Preparation:
15'

Cooking:
0'

Servings:
4

INGREDIENTS

- ½ block feta, cut into 4 (1-inch thick) strips (4-oz)
- ½ cup purple onion, diced
- ½ medium red bell pepper, julienned
- 1 medium cucumber, julienned
- 4 large cherry tomatoes, halved
- 4 large collard green leaves, washed
- 8 whole kalamata olives, halved

- 1 cup full-Fat plain Greek yogurt
- 1 tablespoon white vinegar
- 1 teaspoon garlic powder
- 2 tablespoons minced fresh dill
- 2 tablespoons olive oil
- 2.5-ounces cucumber, seeded and grated (¼-whole)
- Salt and pepper to taste

NUTRITION
Calories: 165.3
Protein: 7.0 gr.
Carbs: 9.9 gr.
Fat: 11.2 gr.

DIRECTIONS:

1. Make the Tzatziki sauce first: make sure to squeeze out all the excess liquid from the cucumber after grating. In a small bowl, mix all sauce ingredients thoroughly and refrigerate.
2. Prepare and slice all wrap ingredients.
3. On a flat surface, spread one collard green leaf. Spread 2 tablespoons of Tzatziki sauce on the middle of the leaf.
4. Layer ¼ of each of the tomatoes, feta, olives, onion, pepper, and cucumber. Place them on the center of the leaf, like piling them high instead of spreading them.
5. Fold the leaf-like you would a burrito. Repeat process for remaining ingredients.
6. Serve and enjoy.

Portobello Mushroom Pizza

Preparation:
20'

Cooking:
12'

Servings:
4

INGREDIENTS

- ½ teaspoon red pepper flakes
- A handful of fresh basil, chopped
- 1 can black olives, chopped
- 1 medium onion, chopped
- 1 green pepper, chopped
- ¼ cup chopped roasted yellow peppers
- ½ cup prepared nut cheese, shredded
- 2 cups prepared gluten-free pizza sauce
- 8 Portobello mushrooms, cleaned and stems removed

NUTRITION
Calories: 578
Carbs: 73.0 gr.
Protein: 24.4 gr.
Fat: 22.4 gr.

DIRECTIONS:

1. Preheat the oven toaster.
2. Take a baking sheet and grease it. Set aside.
3. Place the Portobello mushroom cap-side down and spoon 2 tablespoons of packaged pizza sauce on the underside of each cap. Add nut cheese and top with the remaining ingredients.
4. Broil for 12 minutes or until the toppings are wilted.

Roasted Root Veggies

Preparation:
30'

Cooking:
1 h 30'

Servings:
6

INGREDIENTS

- 2 tbsp olive oil
- 1 head garlic, cloves separated and peeled
- 1 large turnip, peeled and cut into ½-inch pieces
- 1 medium-sized red onion, cut into ½-inch pieces
- 1 ½ lbs. beets, trimmed but not peeled, scrubbed, and cut into ½-inch pieces
- 1 ½ lbs. Yukon gold potatoes, unpeeled, cut into ½-inch pieces
- 2 ½ lbs. butternut squash, peeled, seeded, cut into ½-inch pieces

NUTRITION
Calories: 298
Carbs: 61.1 gr.
Protein: 7.4 gr.
Fat: 5.0 gr.

DIRECTIONS:

1. Grease 2 rimmed and large baking sheets. Preheat oven to 425oF.
2. In a large bowl, mix all ingredients thoroughly.
3. Evenly divide the root vegetables into the two baking sheets and spread in one layer.
4. Season generously with pepper and salt.
5. Pop into the oven and roast for 1 hour and 15 minutes or until golden brown and tender.
6. Remove from oven and let it cool for at least 15 minutes before serving.

Amazingly Good Parsley Tabbouleh

Preparation:
15'

Cooking:
15'

Servings:
4

INGREDIENTS

- ¼ cup chopped fresh mint
- ¼ cup lemon juice
- ¼ tsp salt
- ½ cup bulgur
- ½ tsp minced garlic
- 1 cup water
- 1 small cucumber, peeled, seeded, and diced
- 2 cups finely chopped flat-leaf parsley
- 2 tbsp extra virgin olive oil
- 2 tomatoes, diced
- 4 scallions, thinly sliced
- Pepper to taste

NUTRITION

Calories: 134.8
Carbs: 13 gr.
Protein: 7.2 gr.
Fat: 6 gr.

DIRECTIONS:

1. Cook bulgur according to package instructions. Drain and set aside to cool for at least 15 minutes.
2. Mix pepper, salt, garlic, oil, and lemon juice in a small bowl.
3. Transfer bulgur into a large salad bowl and mix in scallions, cucumber, tomatoes, mint, and parsley.
4. Pour in dressing and toss well to coat.
5. Place bowl in ref until chilled before serving.

Appetizing Mushroom Lasagna

Preparation:
20'

Cooking:
75'

Servings:
8

INGREDIENTS

- No boil lasagna noodles
- ½ cup grated Parmigiano-Reggiano cheese
- Cooking spray
- 3 cups reduced-Fat milk, divided
- ¼ cup all-purpose flour
- 2 tbsp chopped fresh chives, divided
- ½ cup white wine
- 1/3 cup less Fat cream cheese
- 1 ½ tbsp. Chopped fresh thyme
- 6 garlic cloves, minced and divided
- ½ tsp freshly ground black pepper, divided
- 1 package 4 oz pre-sliced exotic mushroom blend
- 1 tsp salt, divided
- 1 package 8oz pre-sliced cremini mushrooms
- 1 ¼ cups chopped shallots
- 2 tbsp olive oil, divided
- 1 oz dried porcini mushrooms
- 1 tbsp butter
- 1 cup boiling water

DIRECTIONS:

1. For 30 minutes, lower porcini in 1 cup extremely hot water with a strainer, strain mushroom, and hold fluid.

2. Over the medium-high fire, liquefy margarine on a skillet. Blend in 2 tbsp oil, and for three minutes, fry shallots. Add ¼ tsp pepper, ½ tsp salt, outlandish mushrooms, and cremini, cook for six minutes. Mix in 3 garlic cloves and thyme, cook briefly. Heat to the point of boiling as you pour wine by expanding fire to high and cook until fluid vanishes for around a moment. Switch off fire and mix in porcini mushrooms, 1 tbsp chives, and cream cheddar. Blend well.

3. On medium-high fire, place a different medium-sized container with 1 tbsp oil. Sauté for a large portion of brief 3 garlic cloves. Then heat to the point of boiling as you pour 2 ¾ cups milk and saved porcini fluid. Season with residual pepper and salt. In a different bowl, whisk together flour and ¼ cup milk and fill skillet. Mix continually and cook until the combination thickens.

4. In a lubed rectangular glass dish, pour and spread ½ cup of sauce, top with lasagna, top with half of the mushroom blend, and one more layer of lasagna. Rehash the layering system and on second thought of the lasagna layer, end with the mushroom blend and cover with cheese.

5. For 45 minutes, bake the lasagna in a preheated 350oF oven. Garnish with chives before serving.

NUTRITION

Calories: 268

Carbs: 29.6 gr.

Protein: 10.2 gr.

Fat: 12.6 gr.

Olives & Tuna Pasta

Preparation:
15'

Cooking:
15'

Servings:
4

INGREDIENTS

- ¼ cup chopped fresh basil
- ¼ cup chopped green olives
- ¼ tsp freshly ground pepper
- ½ cup white wine
- ½ tsp salt, divided
- 2 tbsp lemon juice
- 6-oz whole wheat penne pasta
- 2 tsp freshly grated lemon zest
- 8-oz tuna steak, cut into 3 pieces
- 2 tsp chopped fresh rosemary
- 3 cloves garlic, minced
- 4 tbsp extra virgin olive oil, divided

NUTRITION
Calories: 127.6
Carbs: 13 gr.
Protein: 7.2 gr.
Fat: 5.2 gr.

DIRECTIONS:

1. Cook penne pasta as per bundle directions. Channel and put away.
2. Preheat barbecue to medium-high.
3. In a bowl, throw and blend ¼ tsp pepper, ¼ tsp salt, 1 tsp rosemary, lemon zing, 1 tbsp oil, and fish pieces.
4. Barbecue fish for 3 minutes for each side. Permit to cool and chip into scaled down pieces.
5. Put a huge nonstick pot on medium fire and hotness 3 tbsp oil.
6. Sauté remaining rosemary, garlic olives for 4 minutes
7. Add wine and tomatoes, heat to the point of boiling, and cook for 3 minutes while mixing on occasion.
8. Add staying salt, lemon juice, fish pieces, and pasta. Cook until warmed through.
9. To serve, embellish with basil and appreciate.

Chapter 8

Mediterranean Seafood Recipes

Berries and Grilled Calamari

Preparation:
10'

Cooking:
5'

Servings:
4

NUTRITION
Calories: 567
Fat: 24.5 gr.
Protein: 54.8 gr.
Carbs: 30.6 gr.

INGREDIENTS

- ¼ cup dried cranberries
- ¼ cup extra virgin olive oil
- ¼ cup olive oil
- ¼ cup sliced almonds
- ½ lemon, juiced
- ¾ cup blueberries
- 1 ½ pounds calamari tube, cleaned
- 1 granny smith apple, sliced thinly
- 1 tablespoon fresh lemon juice
- 2 tablespoons apple cider vinegar
- 6 cups fresh spinach
- Freshly grated pepper to taste
- Sea salt to taste

DIRECTIONS:

1. In a small bowl, make the vinaigrette by mixing well the tablespoon of lemon juice, apple cider vinegar, and extra virgin olive oil. Season with pepper and salt to taste. Set aside.
2. Turn on the grill to medium fire and let the grates heat up for a minute or two.
3. In a large bowl, add olive oil and the calamari tube. Season calamari generously with pepper and salt.
4. Place seasoned and oiled calamari onto heated grate and grill until cooked or opaque. This is around two minutes per side.
5. As you wait for the calamari to cook, you can combine almonds, cranberries, blueberries, spinach, and the thinly sliced apple in a large salad bowl. Toss to mix.
6. Remove cooked calamari from the grill and transfer it on a chopping board. Cut into ¼-inch thick rings and throw them into the salad bowl.
7. Drizzle with vinaigrette and toss well to coat the salad.
8. Serve and enjoy!

Delicate Cod Dish

Preparation:
10'

Cooking:
7 h

Servings:
6

NUTRITION
Calories: 119
Carbs: 5.2 gr.
Protein: 21.9 gr.
Fat: 1.5 gr.
Sugar: 3.1 gr.

INGREDIENTS

- 1 lb. cod fillets, cubed
- 1 small onion, sliced 1/2 C. fish broth
- Salt and black pepper, to taste
- 2 large tomatoes, cut into quarters

DIRECTIONS:

1. In a crockpot pot, add cod cubes, onion, garlic, and broth and stir to combine.
2. Set the crockpot on "Low" and cook, covered for about 2 hours. During the last 30 minutes of cooking, stir in the tomatoes.

Versatile Cod

Preparation:
10'

Cooking:
7 h

Servings:
6

NUTRITION
Calories: 119
Carbs: 5 gr.
Protein: 21.7 gr.
Fat: 1.4 gr.
Sugar: 2.6 gr.

INGREDIENTS

- 1 lb. cod fillets, cubed
- 1 medium onion, chopped
- 2 red bell peppers, seeded and cubed
- 1/2 C. homemade fish broth
- Salt and ground black pepper, to taste

DIRECTIONS:

1. In the crockpot, add all the ingredients and stir to combine. Set the crockpot on "Low" and cook, covered for about 6 hours. Uncover the crockpot and serve hot.

Fancy Braeside Shrimp

Preparation:
10'

Cooking:
2 h

Servings:
6

INGREDIENTS

- 1 lb. raw shrimp, peeled and deveined
- 1/4 C. homemade chicken broth
- 3 tbsp. olive oil
- 1 tbsp. fresh lime juice
- Salt and ground black pepper, to taste

NUTRITION
Calories: 227
Carbs: 1.8 gr.
Protein: 26.1 gr.
Fat: 12.5 gr.
Sugar: 0 gr.

DIRECTIONS:

1. In a crockpot, place all the ingredients and stir to combine.
2. Set the crockpot on "High" and cook, covered for about 11/2 hours. Uncover the crockpot and stir the mixture.
3. Serve hot.

Enjoyable Shrimp

Preparation:
10'

Cooking:
7 h

Servings:
6

NUTRITION
Calories: 118
Carbs: 3g
Protein: 22.5 gr.
Fat: 0.2 gr.
Sugar: 3.3 gr.

INGREDIENTS

- 3 C. green bell pepper, seeded and sliced
- 2 C. tomatoes, chopped finely
- 1 C. sugar-free tomato sauce
- Salt and ground black pepper, to taste
- 13/4 lb. large shrimp, peeled and deveined.

DIRECTIONS:

1. In a crockpot, add all ingredients except shrimp and stir to combine. Set the crockpot on "High" and cook, covered for about 2-3 hours. Uncover the crockpot and stir in the shrimp.
2. Set the crockpot on "High" and cook, covered for about 30 minutes. Uncover the crockpot and serve hot.

Cajun Garlic Shrimp Noodle Bowl

Preparation:
15'

Cooking:
15'

Servings:
2

INGREDIENTS

- ½ teaspoon salt
- 1 onion, sliced
- 1 red pepper, sliced
- 4 cherry tomatoes
- 1 teaspoon garlic granules
- 1 tablespoon butter
- 1 teaspoon onion powder
- 2 large zucchinis, cut into noodle
- strips
- 1 teaspoon paprika
- 20 jumbo shrimps, shells removed and deveined
- 3 tablespoon ghee
- 3 cloves garlic, minced
- A dash of cayenne pepper
- A dash of red pepper flakes

NUTRITION
Calories: 712
Carbs: 20.2 gr.
Protein: 97.8 gr.
Fat: 30.0 gr.

DIRECTIONS:

1. Set up the Cajun preparing by blending the onion powder, garlic granules, pepper drops, cayenne pepper, paprika, and salt. Throw in the shrimp to cover in the flavoring.
2. In a skillet, heat the ghee and sauté the garlic. Include the red pepper and onions and continue sautéing for 4 minutes.
3. Add the Cajun shrimp and cook until hazy. Put away.
4. Heat the margarine and sauté the zucchini noodles for three minutes in another container.
5. Assemble by placing the Cajun shrimps on top of the zucchini noodles and tomatoes.

Creamy Bacon-fish Chowder

Preparation:
15'

Cooking:
30'

Servings:
8

NUTRITION
Calories: 400
Carbs: 34.5 gr.
Protein: 20.8 gr.
Fat: 19.7 gr.

INGREDIENTS

- 1 1/2 lbs. cod
- 1 1/2 tsp dried thyme
- 1 large onion, chopped
- 1 medium carrot, coarsely chopped
- 1 tbsp butter, cut into small pieces
- 1 tsp salt, divided
- 3 1/2 cups baking potato, peeled and cubed
- 3 slices uncooked bacon
- 3/4 tsp freshly ground black pepper, divided
- 4 1/2 cups water
- 4 bay leaves
- 4 cups 2% reduced-Fat milk

DIRECTIONS:

1. Add the water and bay leaves in a large skillet and let it simmer. Add the fish. Cover and let it simmer some more until the flesh flakes easily with a fork. Remove the fish from the skillet and cut it into large pieces. Set aside the cooking liquid.
2. Place Dutch oven on medium heat and cook the bacon until crisp. Remove the bacon and reserve the bacon drippings. Crush the bacon and set it aside.
3. Stir potato, onion, and carrot in the pan with the bacon drippings, cook over medium heat for 10 minutes. Add the cooking liquid, bay leaves, 1/2 tsp salt, 1/4 tsp pepper, and thyme, let it boil. Lower the heat and let simmer for 10 minutes. Add the milk and butter, simmer until the potatoes become tender, but do not boil. Add the fish, 1/2 tsp salt, 1/2 tsp pepper. Remove the bay leaves.
4. Serve sprinkled with the crushed bacon.

Cucumber-basil Salsa on Halibut Pouches

Preparation:
15'

Cooking:
17'

Servings:
4

NUTRITION

Calories: 335.4
Carbs: 22.1 gr.
Protein: 20.2 gr.
Fat: 16.3 gr.

INGREDIENTS

- 1 lime, thinly sliced into 8 pieces
- 2 cups mustard greens, stems removed
- 2 tsp olive oil
- 4 – 5 radishes trimmed and quartered
- 4 4-oz skinless halibut filets

- 4 large fresh basil leaves
- Cayenne pepper to taste – optional
- Pepper and salt to taste
- 1 ½ cups diced cucumber
- 1 ½ finely chopped fresh basil leaves
- 2 tsp fresh lime juice
- Pepper and salt to taste

DIRECTIONS:

1. Preheat oven to 400oF.
2. Plan material papers by making 4 bits of 15 x 12-inch square shapes. Longwise, crease fifty-fifty and unfurl pieces on the table.
3. Season halibut filets with pepper, salt, and cayenne-if utilizing cayenne.
4. Just to one side of the overlay going the long way, place ½ cup of mustard greens. Add a basil leaf on the focal point of mustard greens and top with 1 lime cut. Around the greens, layer ¼ of the radishes. Shower with ½ tsp of oil, season with pepper and salt. Top it with a cut of halibut filet.
5. Similarly as you would make a calzone, crease the material paper over your filling and pleat the edges of the material paper starting from one finish to the opposite end. To seal the finish of the pleated material paper, squeeze it.
6. Rehash the cycle to the excess fixings until you have 4 bits of material paper loaded up with halibut and greens.
7. Place pockets in a baking container and prepare in the broiler until halibut is flaky around 15 to 17 minutes.
8. While sitting tight for halibut pockets to cook, make your salsa by blending all salsa fixings in a medium bowl.
9. Whenever halibut is cooked, eliminate it from the stove and make a tear on top. Watch out for the steam as it is extremely hot. Similarly partition salsa and spoon ¼ of salsa on top of halibut through the cut you have made.
10. Serve and enjoy.

Dill Relish on White Sea Bass

Preparation:
15'

Cooking:
12'

Servings:
4

NUTRITION
Calories: 115
Carbs: 12 gr.
Protein: 7gr.
Fat: 1 gr.

INGREDIENTS

- 1 ½ tbsp chopped white onion
- 1 ½ tsp chopped fresh dill
- 1 lemon, quartered
- 4 pieces of 4-oz white sea bass fillets
- 1 tsp Dijon mustard
- 1 tsp lemon juice
- 1 tsp pickled baby capers, drained

DIRECTIONS:

1. Preheat oven to 375oF.
2. Blend lemon juice, mustard, dill, escapades, and onions in a little bowl.
3. Get ready four aluminum foil squares and spot 1 filet for every foil.
4. Press a lemon wedge for every fish.
5. Uniformly partition into 4 the dill spread and sprinkle over the filet.
6. Close the foil over the fish safely and pop it in the broiler.
7. Heat for 10 to 12 minutes or until fish is cooked through.
8. Eliminate from foil and move to a serving platter, serve and appreciate.

Chapter 9

Mediterranean Snack Recipes

Mediterranean Flatbread with Toppings

Preparation:
10'

Cooking:
15'

Servings:
10

NUTRITION
Calories: 101
Carbs: 9 gr.
Protein: 2 gr.
Fat: 6 gr.

INGREDIENTS

- 2 medium tomatoes
- 8 ounces of crescent rolls
- 1 clove of garlic (finely chopped)
- 1 red onion (sliced)
- ¼ tbs. salt

- 4 tbs. olive oil
- ¼ tbs. pepper powder
- 1 and ½ tbs. Italian seasoning
- Parmesan cheese as per requirement

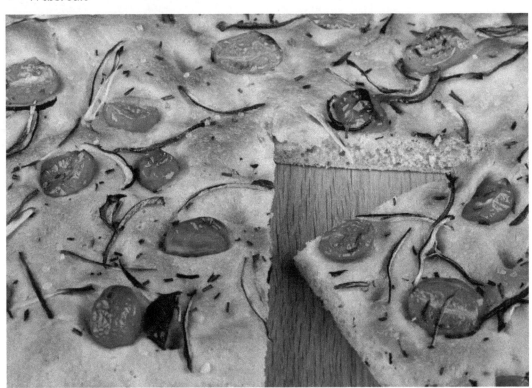

DIRECTIONS:

1. Wash and clean the tomatoes properly. Then make very thin and round slices with a sharp knife. You must ensure that the tomato juices drain out. So, place these on a dry piece of linen cloth.
2. You will get crescent rolls or flatbread dough in the market. Unroll these and keep these on a big baking tray. Make sure the surface of the baking dish has no grease or water.
3. Then roll the dough into several portions, which will not be more than 14x10 inches in measurement.
4. With the help of a rolling pin, shape these into rectangular flatbreads.
5. Place the tomato slices and onion slices on these flatbreads.
6. Add the Italian seasoning, olive oil, pepper powder, salt, and chopped garlic together and mix well.
7. Take the mixture and apply an even coat on all the flatbreads. This mixture will add flavor to the toppings and flatbreads.
8. Put the baking tray in the microwave oven and set the temperature at 375°.
9. After 15 minutes, remove the plate from the oven and enjoy your crunchy Mediterranean flatbread with toppings with a glass of red wine.

Smoked Salmon and Goat Cheese Bites

Preparation:
10'

Cooking:
15'

Servings:
12

NUTRITION
Calories: 739
Carbs: 17.33 gr.
Protein: 54.83 gr.
Fat: 53.33 gr.

INGREDIENTS

- 8 ounces of goat cheese
- 1 tbs. of fresh rosemary
- 2 tbs. of oregano
- 2 tbs. of basil (fresh)

- 2 cloves of garlic (chopped)
- 4 ounces fresh smoked salmon
- ½ tbs. salt
- ½ tbs pepper

DIRECTIONS:

1. People living in Mediterranean love to eat fish, especially Fatty fish like salmon. This is a classic Mediterranean diet snack that combines the smoky flavors of salmon and the sweetness and tanginess of goat cheese.
2. Put the three herbs on the chopping board and run a knife vigorously through them. Once the herbs have been mixed well, transfer them to a medium-sized bowl.
3. Then add goat cheese (grated), chopped garlic, pepper, and salt in the bowl and mix properly. Keep this mixture for some time to rest.
4. There are two ways of serving salmon-goat cheese bites. Either you can place a flat piece of smoked salmon on the tray and top it with a dollop of goat cheese and seasoning mix.
5. The other way is to make small balls with the goat cheese and seasoning mix and wrap a wide stripe of smoked salmon around the ball.
6. To enhance the taste, one can also sprinkle some additional Italian seasoning on the final salmon bites. This step is optional and omitting it will not mar the original richness of the salmon-cheese bites.

Mediterranean Chickpea Bowl

Preparation:
12'

Cooking:
13'

Servings:
2

NUTRITION

Calories: 492

Carbs: 30 gr.

Protein: 12 gr.

Fat: 38 gr.

INGREDIENTS

- ½ tbs. of cumin seeds
- 1 large, julienned carrot
- A ¼ cup of tomatoes (chopped)
- 1 medium julienned zucchini
- A ¼ cup of lemon juice
- 2 sliced green chilies
- ¼ cup of olive oil
- A ½ cup of chopped parsley leaves

- 1 minced clove of garlic
- ¼ tbs. salt
- ¼ tbs. cayenne pepper powder
- A ¼ cup of radish (sliced)
- 3 tbs. walnuts (chopped)
- 1/3 feta cheese (crumbled)
- 1 big can of chickpeas
- Proportionate salad greens

DIRECTIONS:

1. Another ingredient that you will see on the Mediterranean Diet list is chickpeas. The Mediterranean Chickpea Bowl is a popular snack that can be enjoyed at all times. You can use fresh or canned chickpeas as per preference.
2. For the salad, you will have to make a special dressing that will make the dish tasty. You need to roast the cumin seeds in a dry pan. Make sure the heat is medium.
3. When the seeds begin releasing the aroma, put the seeds in a different mixing bowl.
4. Add olive oil, garlic, lemon juice, and tomatoes in this bowl. Also, add the cayenne pepper and salt, and mix well to blend in all the ingredients.
5. Take a big bowl and add the chickpeas into it. Then put in the sliced and chopped veggies and parsley leaves.
6. Adding walnut pieces will add an extra crunch to the Mediterranean chickpea salad.
7. Put in the seasoning you just prepared, and then mix all the ingredients well.

Hummus Snack Bowl

Preparation:
5'

Cooking:
5'

Servings:
2

NUTRITION

Calories: 280

Carbs: 43 gr.

Protein: 12 gr.

Fat: 10 gr.

INGREDIENTS

- 8 tbs of hummus
- ½ cup fresh spinach (coarsely chopped)
- ½ cups of carrots (shredded)
- 1 big tomato (diced)
- ¼ tbs. salt
- ¼ tbs. chili powder
- ¼ tbs. pepper
- 6 sweet olives (3 green, 3 black, chopped)

DIRECTIONS:

1. The Mediterranean Diet will not be complete without the use of hummus. They don't indulge in fast food but opt for fresh salad bowls, which are full of nutrition and goodness.
2. You can either prepare the hummus at home or purchase a jar that does not contain added flavorings and preservatives.
3. Take a large bowl and put 6 spoonful's of hummus into it. In this, put in chopped olives, shredded carrots, spinach leaves, and diced tomatoes.
4. Coat these vegetables with hummus properly.
5. After mixing the vegetables and hummus paste for at least five minutes, add in the chili powder. Make sure that it is evenly spread into the whole salad.
6. Lastly, add pepper powder and salt to the hummus-veggies mixture. You can taste the mixture and check the balance of all the ingredients.
7. Some also drizzle on some extra virgin olive oil onto the salad. This step is optional and can be omitted.
8. The Hummus Snack Bowl is a complete snack on its own. If you desire to add some texture to it, some freshly baked flatbreads or bread will complement the salad.

Crock-Pot Paleo Chunky Mix

Preparation:
5'

Cooking:
1 h 30'

Servings:
2

NUTRITION
Calories: 250
Carbs: 18.6 gr.
Protein: 4 gr.
Fat: 7 gr.

INGREDIENTS

- 4 cups of walnuts (raw and roughly broken)
- 2 cups of cashews (raw and broken in halves)
- 2 cups of plain coconut flakes
- 2/3 cups of sugar granules
- 2 tbs. of olive oil of fresh butter
- 2 tbs. of extracts of vanilla
- 12 ounces of dry banana chips
- 1 and ½ cups of dark chocolate (broken in chips)

DIRECTIONS:

1. As the people of the Mediterranean region love to eat nuts, this is one snack that you will find in each household. It is full of good Fats and gives you energy and healthy bones. The preparation is rather simple, but the cooking process is lengthy.
2. To prepare this dish, you will require a medium-sized crockpot.
3. In this pot, pour in the pieces of walnut, vanilla essence, sugar granules, and olive oil.
4. After this, you must mix the ingredients well and place the pot on high heat.
5. Leave the pot at a high temperature for around 60 minutes.
6. After one hour, you need to reduce the heat to low and cook the mixture for another half an hour.
7. Once the 30 minutes are over, empty the contents of this pot on a dry piece of parchment sheet.
8. After resting the mix for 15 minutes, you need to put the chocolate chips and banana chips.
9. Then mix all these ingredients together. The addition of chocolate will add richness to the sweet and nutty snack.

Smoked Eggplant Dip

INGREDIENTS

Preparation:
20'

Cooking:
40'

Servings:
4

- 1 and a ½ pound of eggplant
- ½ tbsp. pepper powder
- 1 medium coarsely chopped onion
- 4 tbs. of olive oil
- 6 peeled cloves of garlic
- 2 cups of sour cream
- ¾ tbs. salt
- 4 tbs. of lemon juice
- Fresh parsley (minced)
- Liquid smoke (10 drops; optional)

NUTRITION

Calories: 77

Carbs: 5 gr.

Protein: 3 gr.

Fat: 5 gr.

DIRECTIONS:

1. Salads, dressing, and dips are predominant in the Mediterranean diet. But not many are aware that eggplant can be used to make a mean dip that will you change the way you view this versatile vegetable.
2. To start with, you need to peel the outer skin of the eggplants. Using a peeler will come in handy for this task.
3. As a significant part of the cooking will be done in the oven, it is best to preheat it. Crank up the temperature to 400 degrees.
4. Make 1-inch-thick slices of the eggplant. It will ensure the penetration of flavors and even cooking.
5. Take an oven baking tray and brush some olive oil onto the pan. Place the eggplant slices on the pan in an orderly fashion.
6. Sprinkle a thick layer of chopped onions on the eggplant slices. On that, place the cloves of garlic.
7. Roast the veggies inside the oven for 45 minutes. It is best to bring out the tray once and toss the ingredients.
8. Once the slices are evenly cooked and cooled, it is time to make a paste in the blender.
9. When you are happy with the texture of the mixture, add lemon juice and sour cream into it.
10. After mixing all the ingredients, put pepper powder and salt. Adding liquid smoke is optional.
11. After sprinkling in minced fresh parsley leaves, the dip is ready to be consumed with flatbread or banana chips.

Savory Spinach Feta and Sweet Pepper Muffins

Preparation:
10'

Cooking:
25'

Servings:
10

NUTRITION
Calories: 240
Carbs: 15 gr.
Protein: 10 gr.
Fat: 20 gr.

INGREDIENTS

- 2 and ½ cups of flour
- 2 tbs. of baking powder
- A ¼ cup of sugar
- ¾ tbs. salt
- 1 tbs. paprika
- A ¾ cup of milk

- 2 fresh eggs
- ½ cup olive oil
- A ¾ cup of feta (crumbled)
- 1 and ¼ cups of sliced spinach
- 1/3 cup of Florina peppers

DIRECTIONS:

1. If you are looking for a Mediterranean diet snack that will not only fill your belly but will create an explosion of tastes in your mouth, then this is the ultimate option.
2. As the muffins will be baked in the oven, you need to preheat them to a temperature of 190 degrees.
3. Take a deep and large container. In this, put in the sugar, baking powder, salt, and flour. Mix all these dry ingredients properly and make sure there are no lumps.
4. In a separate container, you need to pour in the milk, eggs, and olive oil. Stir these ingredients so that they form one smooth liquid.
5. Carefully pour in the liquids in the container that has the dry ingredients. Use your hand to mix everything well to form a thick and smooth dough.
6. Then it is time to put in the crumbled feta, pepper, and sliced spinach into the dough. Then spend some time with it to ensure that the new ingredients have been mixed evenly into the muffin dough.
7. You can get muffin trays at the market. In such a tray, scoop out portions of the dough and place them into the muffin tray depressions.
8. Put in this pan inside the oven for 25 minutes. After cooling, the muffins will be ready for consumption.

Italian Oven Roasted Vegetables

Preparation:
5'

Cooking:
30'

Servings:
4

NUTRITION

Calories: 100

Carbs: 16 gr.

Protein: 3 gr.

Fat: 4 gr.

INGREDIENTS

- 2 sliced medium onions
- ½ tbs. salt
- 1 tbs. Italian seasoning
- 2 sliced yellow squash
- 1/8 tsp pepper powder
- 3 minced cloves of garlic
- 2 sweet and large yellow and red peppers
- 2 tbs. olive oil

DIRECTIONS:

1. Salads form a big part of the Mediterranean diet. The secret to the health and wellbeing of these people is due to their high vegetable and fruit consumption. If you want to acquire a healthy inner glow, then sacking on these roasted Italian salads will come in handy.
2. Mixing is an art, and the taste of the salad will depend on how well you mix the ingredients.
3. Take all the cut, chopped, minced, and diced vegetables and put them in a large salad mixing bowl.
4. After this, you will have to add the required amounts of salt, Italian seasoning, and pepper powder to the vegetables.
5. Toss these ingredients for some time to ensure that everything has mixed well.
6. Then pour the olive oil into this mixture and again blend well.
7. Place the marinated vegetables in a roasting oven and put them inside the microwave oven.
8. The oven must be preheated at 425-degree temperature. The baking will take no longer than 25 minutes.
9. After pulling out the tray from the oven, you can sprinkle on some extra cheese. This is optional and can be omitted.

Greek Spinach Yogurt Artichoke Dip

Preparation:
10'

Cooking:
10'

Servings:
2

NUTRITION

Calories: 170

Carbs: 20.9 gr.

Protein: 16.3 gr.

Fat: 2.9 gr.

INGREDIENTS

- 1 tbs. olive oil
- 9-ounces spinach (roughly chopped)
- ¼ cup Parmesan cheese (grated)
- 14 ounces artichoke hearts (chopped)
- ½ tbsp. pepper powder

- ½ tbs. onion powder
- ½ tbs. garlic powder
- 8 ounces sliced chestnuts
- 2 cups of Greek yogurt (Fat-free)

DIRECTIONS:

1. Preheat the stove to 350°F.
2. Cleave artichoke hearts into reduced-down pieces. Combine all fixings as one and season with a touch of salt; fill a little goulash or broiler-safe dish (around 1-quart). Sprinkle the top with additional mozzarella cheddar.
3. Prepare for 20-22 minutes, or until warmed through and the cheddar on top is liquefied. Serve warm with pita or tortilla chips.

Chapter 10

Mediterranean Instant Pot Recipes

Kalua Pig

INGREDIENTS

Preparation:
15'

Cooking:
2 h

Servings:
8

- 6 lbs. pork roast, sliced
- 4 bacon slices
- 3 garlic cloves
- 1 cup water
- 1 tablespoon salt
- 1 cabbage, cut into wedges

NUTRITION

Calories: 783

Carbs: 40 gr.

Protein: 5 gr.

Fat: 1 gr.

Fiber: 4 gr.

DIRECTIONS:

1. Set your instant pot to the sauté setting, and cook bacon slices for about 1-minute, cooking and browning all sides. Sprinkle salt on pork. Spread the salt on bacon evenly. Pour water into the instant pot and set to Manual mode.
2. Cover pot with lid and set on high with a cook time of 90-minutes. When the cooking time is completed, set the pot to the "Keep Warm" mode, and release the pressure naturally for 10-minutes. Place the cooked pork in a bowl, taste the remaining liquid in the instant pot. Adjust seasoning as needed.
3. Now chop the cabbage and add it to the instant pot into the cooking liquid. Cover the pot once again and set it on high with a cook time of 5-minutes.
4. When the cooking time is completed, release pressure using quick release. Serve the shredded pork with the cooked cabbage.

Pulled Apart Pork Carnitas

Preparation:
15'

Cooking:
60'

Servings:
6

NUTRITION
Calories: 176
Carbs: 1.3 gr.
Fat: 7 gr.
Fiber: 5 gr.

INGREDIENTS

- 4 lbs. pork roast
- 2 tablespoons olive oil
- 1 head butter lettuce
- 2 grated carrots
- 2 limes, wedge cut
- Water
- 1 tablespoon salt
- 1 tablespoon cocoa

- 1 tablespoon red pepper flakes
- 1 teaspoon cumin
- 1 teaspoon garlic
- 1 teaspoon white pepper
- 2 teaspoons oregano
- 1 large onion, finely chopped
- 1/8 teaspoon cayenne pepper
- 1/8 teaspoon coriander

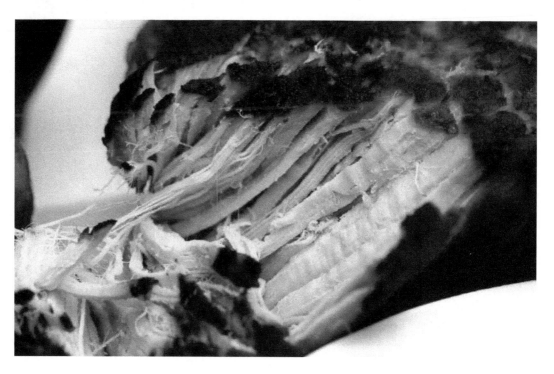

DIRECTIONS:

1. Add the "spice" ingredients to a bowl and mix them well. Season the roast with the prepared mixture and chill the roast in your fridge overnight.
2. Set your instant pot to the sauté mode, add the olive oil, and heat it. Add the meat and brown it well. Add water to the instant pot to submerge meat (about 1 cup).
3. Secure the lid of the pot in place, and set it to Manual mode, on high with a cook time of 60-minutes. When the cooking time is completed, release the pressure naturally for 15-minutes.
4. Remove the meat from the pot and shred the meat from the bones. Set your instant pot to sauté mode, simmer to reduce some of the liquid.
5. Add the shredded pork to a pan set over medium heat and stir-fry them until slightly browned.
6. Add some olive oil and spices.
7. Serve fried pork with the sauce from the instant pot.

Pineapple Pork Chops

Preparation:
15'

Cooking:
30'

Servings:
2

NUTRITION
Calories: 621
Carbs: 101 gr.
Protein: 24 gr.
Fat: 15 gr.

INGREDIENTS

- 1 cup cubed pineapple
- Olive oil as needed
- Seasoning of your choice for pork chops
- Balsamic glaze as required
- 6 pork chops, bone-in

DIRECTIONS:

1. Season the pork chops. Set your instant pot onto the sauté mode.
2. Add the oil and heat it.
3. Add the chops to the pot and sauté them for a 5-minutes.
4. Remove the chops and place them onto a steamer rack for instant pot. Glaze the pork chops and place the pineapple chunks on top of them.
5. Add a cup of water into the instant pot. Secure the lid to the pot and set it to Manual mode, on high with a cook time of 25 minutes.
6. When the cooking time is completed, release the pressure naturally for 10-minutes.

Apple Pork Tenderloins

INGREDIENTS

Preparation:
15'

Cooking:
5'

Servings:
4

NUTRITION
Calories: 123
Carbs: 43 gr.
Protein: 21 gr.
Fat: 45 gr.

- 3 lbs. boneless pork loin roast
- 2 tablespoons butter
- 1 large red onion, thinly sliced
- ½ teaspoon ground black pepper
- ½ teaspoon salt
- ¼ cup chicken broth

- 2 bay leaves
- 4 thyme sprigs, fresh
- 2 medium-sized green apples, sliced

DIRECTIONS:

1. Set your instant pot to the sauté mode, add the butter, and heat it. Add the tenderloin pieces and cook them for 8-minutes.
2. Remove the cooked loins to a serving platter. Place the red onion slices into the pot and sauté for 3-minutes. Stir in the bay leaves, thyme, and apple slices.
3. Add broth along with pepper and salt, stir. Add the loins back to the pot. Secure the pot lid and set it on Manual mode on high with a cook time of 30-minutes.
4. When the cooking time is completed, release the pressure naturally for 10-minutes.
5. Discard the bay leaves and transfer the pork to a cutting board and allow it to sit for 5-minutes.
6. Serve pork with sauce from the pot.

Pork Shoulder Meal

Preparation:
10'

Cooking:
60'

Servings:
6

NUTRITION
Calories: 378
Carbs: 0 gr.
Protein: 48 gr.
Fat: 19 gr.

INGREDIENTS

- 3 lbs. boneless pork shoulder
- Cut into 2-inch cubes
- ¼ cup orange juice
- ¼ cup lime juice
- 5 garlic cloves, minced
- ½ teaspoon cumin, ground

- 1 teaspoon salt
- Chopped cilantro, fresh for garnish

DIRECTIONS:

1. Add your lime juice, orange juice, cumin, garlic, and salt to your instant pot and stir to blend. Place the pork into the instant pot and toss to mix.
2. Secure the lid to the pot and set it to Manual mode, on high with a cook time of 45-minutes. When the cooking time is completed, release the pressure naturally for 10-minutes.
3. Preheat your grill using tongs, take your pork out of the instant pot, and place it on a baking sheet.
4. Set the instant pot to the sauté mode and cook for 10-minutes to allow liquid to reduce. Pour the liquid into a heat-proof dish.
5. Broil the pork for 5-minutes or until crispy and serve with sauce, garnish with fresh cilantro.

Lamb & Feta Cocktail Meatballs

Preparation:
15'

Cooking:
5'

Servings:
10

NUTRITION

Calories: 258

Carbs: 5.3 gr.

Protein: 32.2 gr.

Fat: 11.2 gr.

INGREDIENTS

- 2 garlic cloves, crushed
- 2 lbs. lamb meat, ground
- ½ lb. feta cheese, crumbled
- 1 egg beaten
- ½ cup breadcrumbs
- 2 tablespoons fresh parsley, finely chopped
- 1 tablespoon fresh mint, finely chopped
- ½ teaspoon kosher salt, plus more for sauce
- 1 tablespoon Worcestershire sauce

DIRECTIONS:

1. Add lamb, garlic, feta, egg, breadcrumbs, parsley, mint, salt, pepper, and Worcestershire sauce in a large mixing bowl. Form mixture into 1-inch balls and place them in the freezer; allow them to harden for a few hours.
2. Add 1 cup water and steamer basket to your instant pot. Lower the frozen meatballs onto the steamer basket. Close and secure the lid to the pot.
3. Set on Manual mode, on high, with a cook time of 5-minutes. When the cooking time is completed, release the pressure using the quick release.
4. Serve meatballs on a serving platter, serve with cocktail picks and one of your special sauces.

Instant Pot Lamb Shanks

Preparation:
15'

Cooking:
45'

Servings:
5

NUTRITION
Calories: 377
Carbs: 10 gr.
Fat: 16 gr.
Fiber: 2 gr.

INGREDIENTS

- 3 lbs. lamb shanks
- 1 tablespoon of tomato paste
- 1 large onion, roughly chopped
- 2 celery stalks, roughly chopped
- 2 carrots, medium-sized, roughly chopped

- 2 tablespoons ghee, divided
- Black pepper and salt as needed
- 3 cloves garlic, peeled, smashed
- 1 cup bone broth
- 1 teaspoon Fish Sauce
- 1 tablespoon vinegar

DIRECTIONS:

1. Use salt and pepper to season lamb shanks.
2. Melt a teaspoon of ghee in your instant pot while in the sauté mode. Add the shanks to the pot.
3. Cook for 10-minutes, browning the shanks. Chop vegetables.
4. Remove the lamb from the pot. Add veggies to the pot and season them with some salt and pepper. Add a tablespoon of ghee as well.
5. Once the vegetables are ready, pour garlic clove, tomato paste into the pot and stir. Add in the shanks to veggie mix, along with tomatoes, bone broth, vinegar, and fish sauce.
6. Close and secure lid, set to Manual mode on high, with a cook time of 45-minutes.
7. When the cooking time is completed, release the pressure naturally for 10-minutes.
8. Serve lamb shanks and enjoy!

Inspiring Instant Pot Lamb Stew

Preparation:
15'

Cooking:
40'

Servings:
6

NUTRITION

Calories: 271

Carbs: 5 gr.

Protein: 13 gr.

Fat: 20 gr.

INGREDIENTS

- 2 lbs. lamb stew meat cut up into 1-inch cubes
- 1 acorn squash
- ¼ teaspoon salt
- 6 cloves garlic, sliced
- 1 bay leaf

- 2 sprigs of rosemary
- 1 large yellow onion
- 3 large pieces of carrot

DIRECTIONS:

1. Peel the squash and deseed it, cube the squash. Slice the carrots up into circles. Peel the onion, slice in half, and slice the halves into half-moons.
2. Add all the ingredients into the instant pot, close and secure the pot lid. Set pot to Manual mode, on high, with a cook time of 25-minutes.
3. When the cooking time is completed, release the pressure naturally for 10-minutes.
4. Serve warm and enjoy!

Instant Pot Lamb Spareribs

Preparation:
15'

Cooking:
20'

Servings:
5

NUTRITION

Calories: 165

Carbs: 5 gr.

Fat: 14 gr.

Fiber: 2 gr.

INGREDIENTS

- 2.5 lbs. of pastured lamb spareribs
- 2 teaspoons kosher salt
- 1 tablespoon curry powder
- ½ a pound of minced garlic
- 1 large-sized coarsely chopped onion
- 1 teaspoon of coconut oil
- 4 thinly sliced scallions
- 1 ¼ cup cilantro, divided
- Juice of 1 lemon
- 1 tablespoon kosher salt

DIRECTIONS:

1. Add your spareribs to a bowl. Season them with 2 teaspoons salt, 1 teaspoon of curry powder, and mix well. Coat the ribs thoroughly with the mix.
2. Cover them up and allow them to chill for 4 hours.
3. Set your instant pot to the sauté mode, add oil, and let it heat. Add the spareribs and brown them on both sides for 2-minutes per side.
4. Transfer to another plate.
5. Take a blender and add onion, tomato, and blend into a paste.
6. Add minced garlic to your pot; keep stirring as you add the paste to it. Add curry powder, chopped cilantro, lemon juice, and salt.
7. Let the mixture reach a boil and stir in the ribs.
8. Close and secure the lid to the pot, set it at Manual mode, on high, with a cook time of 20-minutes.
9. When the cooking time is completed, release the pressure naturally for 10-minutes.
10. Serve warm.

Lamb & Avocado Salad

Preparation: 15'

Cooking: 45'

Servings: 10

NUTRITION

Calories: 276

Carbs: 3 gr.

Protein: 21 gr.

Fat: 6 gr.

INGREDIENTS

- 1 avocado, pitted
- 1 cup lettuce
- 1 tablespoon sesame oil
- 1 teaspoon basil
- 1 garlic clove
- 3 tablespoons olive oil
- 1 teaspoon chili pepper
- 1 teaspoon salt
- 3 cups water
- 8-ounces lamb fillet
- 1 cucumber

DIRECTIONS:

1. Place the lamb fillet in the instant pot and add the water. Sprinkle some salt into the pot. Add peeled garlic clove to the lamb mixture.
2. Close the lid to the pot and cook on MEAT mode for 35-minutes.
3. Chop the avocado and slice the cucumber. Combine these ingredients in a mixing bowl. Roughly chop the lettuce and add it to the mixing bowl.
4. Now, sprinkle the mixture with chili pepper, basil, olive oil, and sesame oil.
5. When the meat is done cooking—remove it from your instant pot and chill.
6. Chop the meat roughly and add it to the mixing bowl.
7. Mix up the salad carefully and transfer to a serving bowl.
8. Serve warm.

Beef Stroganoff

Preparation:
15'

Cooking:
15'

Servings:
4

NUTRITION
Calories: 335
Carbs: 12 gr.
Protein: 20.02 gr.
Fat: 18 gr.

INGREDIENTS

- 2 cups of beef strip
- ¼ teaspoon pepper
- ¼ teaspoon salt
- 1 ½ cups zucchini noodles
- 2 cups beef broth
- 3 tablespoons Worcestershire sauce
- 2 tablespoons tomato paste
- 1 cup sliced mushroom
- 2 garlic cloves, minced
- 1 onion, chopped
- 1 tablespoon almond flour
- 3 tablespoon olive oil

DIRECTIONS:

1. In a bowl, mix the beef strips, flour, salt, and pepper.
2. Coat the beef strips with flour and seasoning. Set your instant pot on low heat and low pressure, with a cook time of 10-minutes.
3. Cook your meat for 10-minutes.
4. Place the remaining ingredients into the pot and set for an additional 18-minutes.
5. When the cooking time is completed, release the pressure naturally for 10-minutes.
6. Serve with some zoodles.

Lamb & Feta Meatballs

Preparation:
15'

Cooking:
15'

Servings:
6

INGREDIENTS

- 1 ½ lbs. ground lamb
- 4 garlic cloves, minced
- 1 (28-ounce) can of crushed tomatoes
- 2 tablespoons olive oil
- 2 tablespoons chopped parsley
- ½ cup breadcrumbs
- ½ cup crumbled feta cheese
- 1 onion, chopped

- 1 green bell pepper, chopped
- 1 beaten egg
- 6-ounce can of tomato sauce
- ¼ teaspoon black pepper
- ½ teaspoon salt
- 1 teaspoon oregano, dried
- 1 tablespoon water
- 1 tablespoon mint, fresh, chopped

NUTRITION
Calories: 302
Carbs: 12 gr.
Protein: 30 gr.
Fat: 14 gr.

DIRECTIONS:

1. In a bowl, mix breadcrumbs, egg, lamb, mint, parsley, feta, water, half of the minced garlic, pepper, and salt. Mold into 1-inch balls using your hands. Set your instant pot to the sauté mode, add oil and heat. Add the onion and bell pepper to hot oil and cook for 2-minutes before the rest of the garlic. After about 1-minute, add the crushed tomatoes with their liquid, the tomato sauce, and oregano. Sprinkle with salt and pepper.
2. Close and secure the pot lid, select Manual mode, on high, with a cook time of 8-minutes. When the cooking time is completed, release the pressure using quick release. Serve the meatballs with parsley and more cheese!

Beef Bourguignon

INGREDIENTS

Preparation:
10'

Cooking:
30'

Servings:
4

- 1 lb. of stewing steak
- ½ lb. of bacon
- 1 tablespoon olive oil
- ½ cup beef broth
- 2 teaspoon ground black pepper
- 2 tablespoons fresh parsley, chopped

- 2 tablespoons fresh thyme
- 2 teaspoons rock salt
- 2 garlic cloves, minced
- 1 large peeled and sliced red onion
- 5 medium-sized carrots

NUTRITION

Calories: 416

Carbs: 12 gr.

Protein: 29 gr.

Fat: 18 gr.

DIRECTIONS:

1. Set your instant pot to the sauté mode, add 1 tablespoon of olive oil.
2. Allow the oil to heat, and then add the beef and brown it. Slice the cooked bacon into strips alongside the onion in your pot.
3. Add remaining ingredients and stir. Close and secure the lid, set on Manual, on high, for a cook time of 30-minutes.
4. When the cooking time is completed, release the pressure naturally for 10-minutes.
5. Serve warm and enjoy!

Instant Pot Beef Stew

INGREDIENTS

Preparation:
15'

Cooking:
35'

Servings:
6

- 16-ounces of tenderloin cut
- 1 piece of chopped onion
- 3 Yukon gold potatoes, chopped up
- 1 zucchini, chopped
- 1 cup carrots, chopped
- 2 cups beef broth
- 2 teaspoon sea salt
- 1 piece of bay leaf

- 1 tablespoon tomato paste
- 1 teaspoon onion powder
- 1 teaspoon paprika
- 1 teaspoon pepper
- 2 tablespoons arrowroot flour
- Worcestershire sauce

NUTRITION
Calories: 310
Carbs: 18 gr.
Protein: 39 gr.
Fat: 8 gr.

DIRECTIONS:

1. Set your instant pot to the sauté mode, add the oil, and heat it. Add the tenderloin to the oil. Sauté them until the meat is well cooked and no longer pink.
2. Add the vegetables and stir in the broth with seasoning. Close and secure the lid, set to STEW/MEAT mode, with a cook time of 35-minutes.
3. Once cook time is completed, release the pressure naturally for 10-minutes.
4. Ladle ¼ of the liquid into a bowl and mix arrowroot flour with it, making a slurry.
5. Add the slurry back into the instant pot and stir.
6. Season a bit with salt, serve hot and enjoy!

Simple Beef Short Ribs

Preparation:
10'

Cooking:
15'

Servings:
5

NUTRITION
Calories: 440
Carbs: 10 gr.
Protein: 27 gr.
Fats: 41 gr.

INGREDIENTS

- 4lbs. beef short ribs
- 1 tablespoon of beef Fat
- 3 cloves garlic
- ½ cup water
- 1 quartered onion
- Generous amount of kosher salt

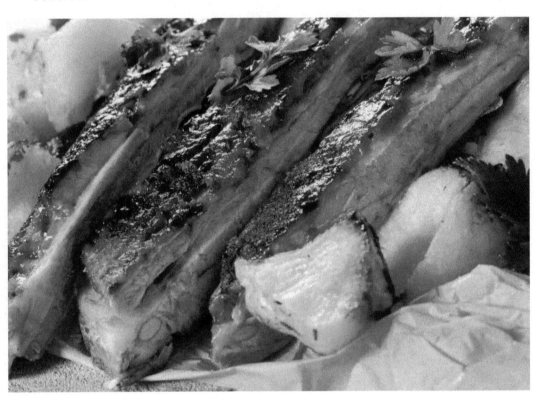

DIRECTIONS:

1. Season the beef ribs with salt all over. In a skillet, over medium heat, add oil and allow it to heat up.
2. Add the ribs to the skillet and brown them. Add the onion, garlic, and water.
3. Transfer the mixture to your instant pot and stir. Close and secure the lid, set on Manual mode, on high, with a cook time of 35-minutes.
4. Release the pressure naturally for 10-minutes.
5. Serve warm.

Chicken & Tomato Soup

Preparation:
15'

Cooking:
35'

Servings:
6

NUTRITION
Calories: 287
Carbs: 6 gr.
Protein: 26 gr.
Fat: 11 gr.

INGREDIENTS

- 1 tablespoon olive oil
- Black pepper to taste
- Salt to taste
- 15-ounces chicken broth
- 15-ounces tomatoes, diced
- 1 teaspoon oregano, dried
- 1 teaspoon thyme, dried
- 1 tablespoon garlic, minced
- 1 medium onion, chopped
- 1 lb. lean ground chicken

DIRECTIONS:

1. Set your instant pot to the sauté mode, add the oil, and heat it.
2. Cook chicken until the meat turns brown. Add onion, thyme, garlic, and oregano and cook for 3-minutes.
3. Add the tomatoes and chicken broth and close the pot lid.
4. Set the pot on the SOUP mode and cook for 30-minutes.
5. When the cooking is completed, release the pressure using the quick release. Serve soup warm.

Chicken Chili from Instant Pot

Preparation:
15'

Cooking:
30'

Servings:
10

INGREDIENTS

- 2 lbs. ground chicken
- 2 tablespoons olive oil
- 2 red onions, diced
- 10 garlic cloves, minced
- 8 carrots, chopped
- 5 celery stalks, chopped
- 2 bell peppers, chopped
- 2 teaspoons salt
- 1 tablespoon cumin
- 1 tablespoon oregano
- 2 tablespoons chili powder
- 14-ounces tomatoes, diced
- 2 jalapenos, minced
- 1 teaspoon black pepper
- ¼ teaspoon cayenne

NUTRITION
Calories: 296
Carbs: 7 gr.
Protein: 28 gr.
Fat: 12 gr.

DIRECTIONS:

1. Set your instant pot to the sauté mode, add the oil, and heat it. Add the oil and garlic and sauté them for a few minutes.
2. Add the chicken and brown the chicken.
3. Place the remaining ingredients into the pot and place the lid on the pot. Set on the BEAN/CHILI mode, and it will automatically cook for 30-minutes.
4. When cook time is over, release the pressure naturally for 10-minutes.
5. Garnish with fresh chopped cilantro and serve warm.

Chicken Soup

Preparation:
15'

Cooking:
30'

Servings:
8

NUTRITION
Calories: 296
Carbs: 8 gr.
Protein: 27 gr.
Fat: 9 gr.

INGREDIENTS

- 1.5 lbs. chicken drumsticks
- 1-quart chicken stock
- ½ teaspoon cracked black pepper
- 2 bay leaves
- 1 small yellow onion, diced
- 1 medium rutabaga, diced
- 1 large parsnip, diced
- 2 medium carrots, diced
- 2 large celery ribs, sliced

DIRECTIONS:

1. Add all the ingredients into an instant pot and pour the chicken stock over them. Close the lid to the pot, set the pot on the SOUP setting.
2. Once the cooking time is completed, release the pressure naturally.
3. Remove the chicken pieces and bones.
4. Transfer meat back to the pot and adjust seasoning if needed.
5. Serve the soup warm.

Chicken Curry with Lemon & Coconut

Preparation:
15'

Cooking:
40'

Servings:
6

NUTRITION
Calories: 289
Carbs: 9 gr.
Protein: 29 gr.
Fat: 13 gr.

INGREDIENTS

- 1 can coconut milk
- ¼ cup lemon juice
- 1 teaspoon lemon zest
- 4 lb. chicken breast
- ½ teaspoon salt
- 1 teaspoon turmeric

DIRECTIONS:

1. In a bowl, add lemon juice, the liquid portion of coconut milk, lemon zest, and all the spices to make the marinade mixture.
2. Coat the chicken pieces with the mixture and then set them aside.
3. Pour half the portion of coconut milk into an instant pot, add marinated chicken to the pot.
4. Pour remaining coconut milk over the chicken and close the lid to the pot. Set to the POULTRY setting and cook for 20-minutes.
5. When the cooking time is completed, release the pressure using the quick release.
6. Serve the chicken warm as a side dish.

Chicken Drumsticks in Tomato Sauce

Preparation:
15'

Cooking:
30'

Servings:
3

NUTRITION
Calories: 302
Carbs: 10 gr.
Protein: 32 gr.
Fat: 13 gr.

INGREDIENTS

- 6 chicken drumsticks
- 1 tablespoon cider vinegar
- 1.5 cups tomatillo sauce
- 1 teaspoon olive oil
- 1 teaspoon oregano, dried
- 1/8 teaspoon black pepper
- 1 teaspoon salt
- ¼ cup chopped cilantro
- 1 jalapeno, halved and seeded

DIRECTIONS:

1. Season the chicken with salt, vinegar, pepper, oregano and marinate them for 2-hours.
2. Set your instant pot to the sauté mode, add the oil, and heat it.
3. Sauté the chicken until the meat is browned. After frying the chicken, add all the other ingredients (except for the cilantro) and shut the lid to the pot.
4. Set on Manual mode on high, with a cook time of 20-minutes.
5. When the cooking time is completed, release the pressure using quick release.
6. Garnish with chopped cilantro just before serving.

Chapter 11

Mediterranean Dessert Recipes

Ekmek Kataifi

Preparation:
30'

Cooking:
45'

Servings:
10

NUTRITION
Calories: 649
Carbs: 37 gr.
Protein: 11 gr.
Fat: 52 gr.

INGREDIENTS

- 1 cup of water
- 1 cup of sugar
- 2 (2-inch) strips lemon peel, pith removed
- ½ cup plus 1 tbsp. unsalted butter, melted
- 1 tbsp. fresh lemon juice
- ½lbs. frozen kataifi pastry, thawed, at room temperature
- 2 ½ cups whole milk
- 2 large eggs
- ½ tsp. ground mastiha
- ¼ cup fine semolina
- 1 tsp. of cornstarch
- ¼ cup of sugar
- 1 tsp. vanilla extract
- ½ cup sweetened coconut flakes
- 1 cup whipping cream
- 1 tsp. powdered milk
- ½ cup chopped unsalted pistachios

DIRECTIONS:

1. Set the oven to 350°F. Oil the baking container with 1. Tbsp of margarine.
2. Put a pot on medium hotness, then add water, sugar, lemon juice, lemon strip. Pass on to bubble for around 10 minutes. Hold.
3. Unravel the kataifi, cover with the extra margarine, then, at that point, place in the baking dish.
4. Blend the milk and mastiha, then put it on medium hotness. Eliminate from heat when the milk is scalded, then, at that point, cool the blend.
5. Blend the eggs, cornstarch, semolina, and sugar in a bowl, mix completely, then whisk the cooled milk combination into the bowl.
6. Move the egg and milk combination to a pot and put on heat. Sit tight for it to thicken like custard, then, at that point, add the coconut drops and cover it with a cling wrap. Cool.
7. Spread the cooled custard-like material over the kataifi. Place in the fridge for somewhere around 8 hours.
8. Decisively eliminate the kataifi from the skillet with a blade. Eliminate it so that the shape faces up.
9. Whip a cup of cream, add 1 tsp. vanilla, 1tsp. powdered milk, and 3 tbsps. Of sugar. Spread the blend all around the custard, sit tight for it to solidify, then flip and add the extra cream combination to the kataifi side.
10. Serve.

Revani Syrup Cake

Preparation:
30'

Cooking:
3 h

Servings:
24

NUTRITION

Calories: 348

Carbs: 55 gr.

Protein: 5 gr.

Fat: 9 gr.

INGREDIENTS

- 2 tbsps. all-purpose flour
- 1 tbsp. unsalted butter
- 1 cup ground rusk or breadcrumbs
- ¾ cup ground toasted almonds
- 1 cup fine semolina flour
- 16 large eggs
- 3 tsp baking powder

- 2 tbsps. vanilla extract
- 3 cups of sugar, divided
- 5 (2-inch) strips lemon peel, pith removed
- 3 cups of water
- 1 oz of brandy
- 3 tbsps. fresh lemon juice

DIRECTIONS:

1. Preheat the oven to 350°F. Oil the baking skillet with 1 Tbsp. of margarine and flour.
2. Blend the rusk, almonds, semolina, baking powder in a bowl.
3. In another bowl, blend the eggs, 1 cup of sugar, vanilla, and whisk with an electric blender for around 5 minutes. Add the semolina combination to the eggs and mix.
4. Empty the blended player into the lubed baking container and spot it in the preheated oven.
5. Make the syrup with the excess sugar, lemon strips, and water by heating up the combination on medium hotness. Add the lemon juice following 6 minutes, then cook for 3 minutes. Eliminate the lemon strips and put the syrup away.
6. After the cake is done in the oven, spread the syrup over the cake.
7. Cut the cake however you see fit serve.

Kourabiedes Almond Cookies

Preparation:
20'

Cooking:
50'

Servings:
20

NUTRITION

Calories: 102
Carbs: 10 gr.
Protein: 2 gr.
Fat: 7 gr.

INGREDIENTS

- 1 ½ cups unsalted butter, clarified, at room temperature
- 1 large egg yolk
- Confectioners' sugar, divided
- 1 1/2 tsp baking powder
- 2 tbsps. brandy
- 5 cups all-purpose flour, sifted
- 1 tsp vanilla extract
- 1 cup roasted almonds, chopped

DIRECTIONS:

1. Preheat the oven to 350°F
2. Completely blend margarine and ½ cup of sugar in a bowl. Add in the egg after a while. Make a cognac blend by blending the liquor and baking powder. Add the combination to the egg, add vanilla, then continue to beat until the ingredients are properly blended.
3. Add flour and almonds to make a mixture.
4. Roll the dough to form crescent shapes. You ought to have the option to get around 40 pieces. Put the pieces on a baking sheet, then heat in the oven for 25 minutes.
5. Permit the treats to cool, then cover them with the leftover confectioner's sugar.
6. Serve.

Crème Caramel

Preparation:
1 h

Cooking:
1 h

Servings:
12

NUTRITION
Calories: 110
Carbs: 21 gr.
Protein: 2 gr.
Fat: 1 gr.

INGREDIENTS

- 5 cups of whole milk
- 2 tsp vanilla extract
- 8 large egg yolks
- 4 large-sized eggs
- 2 cups sugar, divided
- ¼ cup Of water

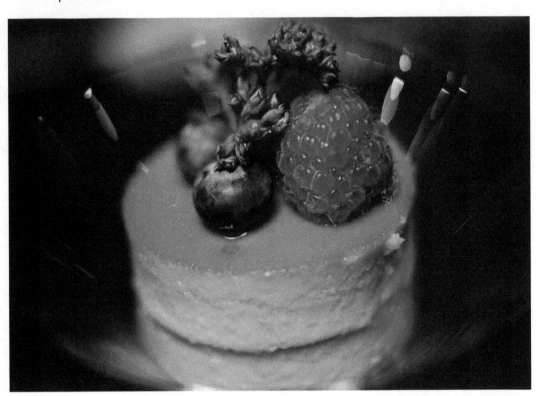

DIRECTIONS:

1. Preheat the oven to 350°F
2. Heat the milk on medium hotness until it is scalded.
3. Blend 1 cup of sugar and eggs in a bowl and add them to the eggs.
4. With a nonstick pan on high hotness, heat up the water and remaining sugar. Do not stir; instead, whirl the pan. When the sugar forms caramel, divide it into ramekins.
5. Partition the egg blend into the ramekins and spot them in a baking dish. Add water to the skillet until it is half full. Heat for 30 minutes.
6. Eliminate the ramekins from the baking skillet, cool, then refrigerate for no less than 8 hours.

Galaktoboureko

INGREDIENTS

Preparation:
30'

Cooking:
90'

Servings:
12

- 1 tbsp. fresh lemon juice
- 4 cups sugar, divided
- Tbsps. vanilla extract
- 1 cup of water
- Room temperature whole milk
- 1 cup plus 2 tbsps. unsalted butter, melted, and divided into 2

- 1 Tbsp. plus 1 ½ tsp grated lemon zest, divided into 10 cups
- 7 large-sized eggs
- 1 cup of fine semolina
- 1 package phyllo, thawed and at room temperature

NUTRITION
Calories: 393
Carbs: 55 gr.
Protein: 8 gr.
Fat: 15 gr.

DIRECTIONS:

1. Preheat oven to 350°F
2. Blend 2 cups of sugar, lemon juice, 1 ½ tsp of lemon zing, and water. Bubble over medium hotness. Put away.
3. Blend the milk, 2 Tbsps. of spread and vanilla in a pot and put on medium hotness. Eliminate from heat when milk is scalded.
4. Blend the eggs and semolina in a bowl, then add the combination to the singed milk. Put the egg-milk blend on medium hotness. Mix until it frames a custard-like material.
5. Brush butter on each sheet of phyllo and arrange it all over the baking pan until everywhere is covered. Spread the custard on the bottom pile of phyllo
6. Organize the buttered phyllo all around the highest point of the custard until each inch is covered.
7. Heat for around 40 minutes. Cover the highest point of the pie with all the pre-arranged syrup. Serve.

Loukoumades (Fried Honey Balls)

Preparation:
20'

Cooking:
45'

Servings:
10

INGREDIENTS

- 1 cup of water
- 2 cups of sugar
- 1 ½ cups tepid water
- 1 cup honey
- 1 tbsp. active dry yeast
- 1 tbsp. brown sugar
- ¼ cup of vegetable oil
- 1 ½ cups all-purpose flour

- ½ tsp salt
- 1 cup cornstarch
- Vegetable oil for frying
- 1 ½ cups chopped walnuts
- ¼ cup ground cinnamon

NUTRITION

Calories: 355
Carbs: 64 gr.
Protein: 6 gr.
Fat: 7 gr.

DIRECTIONS:

1. Heat up the sugar and water on medium hotness. Add honey following 10 minutes. Cool and put away.
2. Blend the lukewarm water, oil, sugar,' and yeast in an bowl. Permit it to sit for 10 minutes. In another bowl, blend the flour, salt, and cornstarch. With your hands, blend the yeast and the flour to make a wet mixture. Cover and put away for 2 hours.
3. Sear in oil at 350°F. Utilize your palm to quantify the measures of the mixture as they are dropped into the griddle. Broil each clump for around 3-4 minutes.
4. Promptly the loukoumades are finished searing, drop them in the syrup.
5. Present with cinnamon and pecans.

Pear Croustade

Preparation:
30'

Cooking:
60'

Servings:
10

NUTRITION

Calories: 498

Carbs: 32 gr.

Protein: 18 gr.

Fat: 32 gr.

INGREDIENTS

- 1 cup plus 1 tbsp. all-purpose flour, divided
- 4 ½ tbsps. sugar, divided
- 1/8 tsp salt
- 6 tbsps. unsalted butter, chilled, cut into ½ inch cubes
- 1 large-sized egg, separated
- 1 and ½ tbsps. ice-cold water
- 3 firm, ripe pears (Bosc), peeled, cored, sliced into ¼ inch slices
- 1 tsp anise seeds
- 1/3 tsp ground allspice
- 1 tbsp. fresh lemon juice

DIRECTIONS:

1. Pour 1 cup of flour, 1 ½ Tbsps. of sugar, spread, and salt into a food processor and join the fixings by beating.
2. Whisk the yolk of the egg and ice water in a different bowl. Blend the egg combination in with the flour combination. It will shape a batter, wrap it, and put away for 60 minutes.
3. Set the stove to 400°F.
4. Blend the pear, sugar, extra flour, allspice, anise seed, and lemon juice in a bowl to make a filling.
5. Arrange the filling on the focal point of the batter.
6. Bake for around 45 minutes. Cool for around 15 minutes prior to serving

Melomakarona

Preparation:
20'

Cooking:
45'

Servings:
20'

NUTRITION
Calories: 294
Carbs: 44 gr.
Protein: 3 gr.
Fat: 12 gr.

INGREDIENTS

- 4 cups of water
- 4 cups of sugar, divided
- 1 cup plus 1 tbsp. honey, divided
- 1 cinnamon stick
- 1 (2-inch) strip orange peel, pith removed
- ½ cup extra-virgin olive oil
- ¼ cup Metaxa brandy or any other brandy
- ¼ cup unsalted butter,
- 1 tbsp. grated

- ¾ cup of orange juice
- Orange zest
- ¾ cup fine semolina flour
- 1 tsp ground cloves, divided
- ¼ tsp baking soda
- 3 cups pastry flour
- 1 ½ tsp baking powder
- 4 tsp ground cinnamon, divided
- 1/2 cups finely chopped walnuts
- 1/3 cup brown sugar

DIRECTIONS:

1. Blend 3 ½ cups of sugar, 1 cup honey, orange strip, cinnamon stick, and water in a pot and hotness it for around 10 minutes.
2. Blend the sugar, oil, and spread for about minutes, then, at that point, add the cognac, extra honey, and zing. Then, at that point, add a combination of baking soda and orange juice . Blend completely.
3. In a different bowl, blend the cake flour, baking powder, semolina, 2 tsp of cinnamon, and ½ tsp. of cloves. Add the blend to the blender gradually. Run the blender until the fixings structure a batter. Cover and put away for 30 minutes.
4. Set the stove to 350°F
5. With your palms, structure little oval balls from the batter. Make a total of forty balls.
6. Bake the cookie balls for 30 minutes, then, at that point, drop them in the pre-arranged syrup.
7. Make a combination of pecans, extra cinnamon, and cloves. Spread the blend on the highest point of the prepared treats.
8. Serve the treats or store them in a shut cover compartment.

Feta Cheesecake

INGREDIENTS

Preparation:
30'

Cooking:
90'

Servings:
12

NUTRITION

Calories: 98

Carbs: 7 gr.

Protein: 3 gr.

Fat: 7 gr.

- 2 cups graham cracker crumbs (about 30 crackers)
- 6 tbsps. unsalted butter, melted
- 12 ounces cream cheese, softened
- ½ tsp ground cinnamon
- ½ cup sesame seeds, toasted
- 1 cup crumbled feta cheese
- 2 cups plain yogurt
- 3 large eggs
- 1 cup of sugar
- 2 tbsps. grated lemon zest
- 1 tsp vanilla

DIRECTIONS:

1. Set the oven to 350°F.
2. Blend the saltine scraps, margarine, cinnamon, and sesame seeds with a fork. Move the combination to a springform pan and spread until it is even. Refrigerate.
3. In a different bowl, blend the cream cheddar and feta. With an electric blender, beat the two sorts of cheddar together. Add the eggs in a steady progression, beating the combination with each new option. Add sugar, then continue to beat until velvety. Blend in yogurt, vanilla, and lemon zing.
4. Bring out the refrigerated springform and spread the batter on it. Then place it in a baking container. Fill the baking container with water until it is mostly full.
5. Bake for about 50 minutes. Remove cheesecake and allow it to cool. Refrigerate for at least 4 hours.
6. It is done. Serve when ready.

Stuffed Dried Figs

Preparation:
20'

Cooking:
0'

Servings:
4

NUTRITION

Calories: 110

Carbs: 26 gr.

Protein: 1 gr.

Fat: 3 gr.

INGREDIENTS

- 12 dried figs
- 24 walnut halves
- 2 Tbsps. thyme honey
- 2 Tbsps. sesame seeds

DIRECTIONS:

1. Cut off the tough stalk ends of the figs.
2. Cut open every fig.
3. Stuff the fig openings with two pecan parts and close
4. Organize the figs on a plate, shower with honey, and sprinkle the sesame seeds on it.
5. Serve.

Conclusion

The Mediterranean diet isn't just a way to eat; it's a way to love eating. Commit to following the diet and following the example of a culture where fresh, seasonal ingredients are respected and prized, where meals are simply prepared and generously shared, and where time is spent lingering over food, wine, and conversation.

Eating the Mediterranean way cannot just work on your wellbeing and assist you with shedding pounds; it can likewise urge you to dial back, no less than a few times each day, and enjoy some time off from a furious timetable and a bustling life.

Have a great time investigating the Mediterranean eating routine; appreciate going through the ends of the week at your neighborhood ranchers' market and making an undertaking out of attempting new fixings. Incorporate a more friendly time into your week by imparting these straightforward yet delectable dishes to your loved ones.

The Mediterranean diet isn't just about healthful living; it's about joyful living!

CPSIA information can be obtained
at www.ICGtesting.com
Printed in the USA
BVHW061800160822
644714BV00007BA/371